# Improving Induction

## Research-based best practice for schools

## Sara Bubb, Ruth Heilbronn, Cath Jones, Michael Totterdell and Maxine Bailey

London and New York

First published 2002
by RoutledgeFalmer
11 New Fetter Lane, London EC4P 4EE

Simultaneously published in the USA and Canada
by RoutledgeFalmer
29 West 35th Street, New York, NY 10001

*RoutledgeFalmer is an imprint of the Taylor & Francis Group*

© 2002 Sara Bubb, Ruth Heilbronn, Cath Jones, Michael
Totterdell and Maxine Bailey

Typeset in Times by
Wearset Ltd, Boldon, Tyne and Wear
Printed and bound in Great Britain by
Cromwell Press, Trowbridge, Wiltshire

*British Library Cataloguing in Publication Data*
A catalogue record for this book is available from the British
Library

*Library of Congress Cataloging in Publication Data*
A catalog record for this book has been requested

ISBN 0–415–27780–9

# Contents

# Figures

# Tables

# Boxes

# Contributors

**Sara Bubb** trains NQTs and induction tutors throughout England, Wales and Jersey and co-ordinates the employment-based routes to QTS at the Institute. She has written three books and has an advice column for new teachers in the *TES*. She is an OFSTED inspector, threshold assessor and external assessor for the TTA.

**Ruth Heilbronn** has worked in the field of induction at school, LEA and HEI level. She runs sessions on mentoring new teachers and overseas teacher educators, particularly focusing on monitoring and assessment. She works on the PGCE and Masters of Teaching programme at the Institute.

**Cath Jones** is a Research Officer at the Institute of Education and has worked on various projects in the areas of education policy analysis and sociology of education.

**Michael Totterdell** is Dean of Initial Teacher Education at the Institute. He has worked with schools and government agencies and non-government organisations in the UK and abroad to develop the partnership model of teacher education. He is Vice Chair of UCET, an OFSTED Inspector and Churchill Fellow.

**Maxine Bailey** was a research officer on the induction research project at the Institute of Education. She has also worked for NfER and now works for the DfES in the curriculum division.

# Acknowledgements

This research was supported by a number of people. The research team would like to express their thanks to the steering group, which included members of the DfES, TTA, OFSTED, GTC and HMI.

The authors wish to offer special thanks to all the schools and individuals involved in the research, for talking to us and sharing their experiences of and views on the statutory induction year.

Acknowledgement is made of the help of colleagues, Peter Earley and Barbara MacGilchrist, who offered invaluable advice during the project. We wish to thank Lilah Heilbronn for research support and all the administrative staff involved with the project for their invaluable support. Finally, we thank the Institute of Education for hosting this research project.

Most of all, we thank our family and friends for their encouragement and tolerance while we wrote this book. Special mention goes to Paul, Julian, Miranda and Oliver.

From September 2000 to December 2001 we carried out a research project for the DfES, as reported in *Evaluation of the Effectiveness of the Statutory Arrangements for the Induction of Newly Qualified Teachers*, Research Brief and Report no. 338, DfES: London. Some of the material in this book, such as the Main Findings in Chapter One, draws on this research and is published with the permission of the DfES, on behalf of Her Majesty's Stationery Office. Applications for reproduction of this material should be made in writing to The Crown Copyright Unit, Her Majesty's Stationery Office, St Clemens House, 2–16 Colegate, Norwich, NR3 1BQ.

# Abbreviations

| | |
|---|---|
| AB | Appropriate Body |
| AST | Advanced Skills Teacher |
| ATL | Association of Teachers and Lecturers |
| B.Ed | Bachelor of Education |
| CEP | Career Entry Profile |
| CPD | Continuing Professional Development |
| CTC | City Technology College |
| DfEE | Department for Education and Employment |
| DfES | Department for Education and Skills |
| FEFC | Further Education Funding Council |
| GCSE | General Certificate of Secondary Education |
| GTC | General Teaching Council (for England) |
| HEFCE | Higher Education Funding Council for England |
| HEI | Higher Education Institution |
| HMI | Her Majesty's Inspectorate |
| ICT | Information and Communications Technology |
| IEP | Individual Education Plan |
| INSET | In-Service Education and Training |
| ISCTIP | Independent Schools Council Teacher Induction Panel |
| ITE | Initial Teacher Education |
| ITT | Initial Teacher Training |
| LEA | Local Education Authority |
| LGA | Local Government Association |
| LPSH | Leadership Programme for Serving Headteachers |
| NPQH | National Professional Qualification for Headship |
| NQT | Newly Qualified Teacher |
| NUT | National Union of Teachers |
| OFSTED | Office for Standards in Education |
| PEIY | Project on the Effectiveness of the Induction Year |
| PGCE | Postgraduate Certificate in Education |
| QCA | Qualifications and Curriculum Authority |

| | |
|---|---|
| QTS | Qualified Teacher Status |
| SCITT | School-Centred Initial Teacher Training |
| SEN | Special Educational Needs |
| SENCO | Special Educational Needs Co-ordinator |
| SFC | Sixth Form College |
| SMART | Specific, Measurable, Achievable, Relevant, Time bound |
| TIAC | Teacher Induction Appeal Committee |
| *TES* | *Times Educational Supplement* |
| TTA | Teacher Training Agency |

# Chapter 1

# Introduction

## The structure of the book

This book contains two inter-related elements: the findings from our research and ideas and examples of good practice. We look first at the induction regulations to consider what is supposed to happen and then discuss why we need a statutory induction period. We then look at how schools manage induction and consider how it is organised in distinctive settings. Later we consider what effective induction tutors do and then how to get the most from Appropriate Bodies. The Career Entry Profile and the process of setting objectives are explored and we look at how NQTs use their 10 per cent reduction in timetable. Towards the end of the book we give ideas for how to observe and assess NQTs against the induction standards. The book concludes with a chapter linking induction to further professional development.

## The regulations for statutory induction

The regulations for the statutory induction period were originally laid out in Circular 5/99 (DfEE 1999) but there have been several updates: 90/2000 (DfEE 2000a), 582/2001; (DfES 2001f). The most up-to-date version is on the DfES website (URL: www.dfes.gov.uk).

The policy regulations state that all people who are awarded QTS after 7 May 1999 have to complete a statutory induction period of a school year, to teach in maintained schools in England. The policy was introduced to provide:

- all newly qualified teachers with a bridge from initial teacher education to effective professional practice,
- a foundation for the long-term continuing professional development of new teachers,
- well-targeted support, which in turn helps newly qualified teachers to

make a real and sustained contribution to school improvement and to raising classroom standards.

(DfEE 2000a: para.1)

The policy has two main principles:

- a national entitlement for NQTs to support and professional development,
- assessment of NQTs against defined national standards.

Thus, it can be seen as a 'carrot and stick' or pressure and support style of policy. On the one hand, NQTs must be assessed by their school at the end of each of the three terms that make up the induction period. On the other hand, the government intend induction to be 'a bridge from initial teacher training to effective professional practice' (DfEE 2000a: para.1). It is intended to give NQTs reduced timetable and a framework of monitoring, support and assessment. NQTs who are doing well perceive the assessment meetings and reports as a carrot. They are, however, a stick for those who are having problems. No longer should a successful first year of teaching be a matter of luck and favours. It is an entitlement that has been planned and funded, and which head teachers are required by law to provide. NQTs should have the following package of opportunities and requirements:

1 a 10 per cent lighter teaching timetable than other teachers in the school,
2 a job description that does not make unreasonable demands,
3 meetings with a school 'induction tutor', including half termly reviews of progress,
4 an individualised programme of support, monitoring and assessment,
5 objectives, informed by strengths and areas for development identified in the career entry profile, to help them meet the induction standards,
6 at least one observation of their teaching each half term with oral and written feedback,
7 an assessment meeting and report at the end of each term,
8 procedures to air grievances at school and local education authority level.

The timeline in Figure 1.1 indicates the key stages in the induction period as set out in the induction circular.

## Who must complete the statutory induction period?

People who were awarded Qualified Teacher Status (QTS) after 7 May 1999 have to complete an induction period of a school year (or equivalent) if they are to work in maintained primary or secondary schools, or in non-maintained special schools in England. Those who qualified before May 1999 do not have to go through statutory induction, even if they do not take up their first post until after September 1999.

Only teachers with QTS are entitled to induction. Those who have teaching qualifications outside the European Union have to gain QTS in England through the Overseas Trained Teacher Scheme.

Teachers do not, by law, have to complete an induction year if they work in the independent sector, though they would need to if they moved to the state sector. However, they can complete their induction period in an independent school if it teaches to the National Curriculum. The Independent Schools' Council recommends that their members provide induction.

Supply teachers can only start their induction period if they are employed for a full term to teach the same class. NQTs can only work as short-term supply teachers for a year and a term after their first appointment, before taking a settled job in which to do their induction. This should benefit teachers because they will get the support and further training that they need.

## Where can NQTs complete their induction period?

All state schools in England must provide an induction period. For others it is optional, so that the following can provide induction if they wish:

a   non-maintained special schools,
b   independent schools, if they teach the National Curriculum,
c   sixth form colleges – no more than 10 per cent of NQTs' teaching should be devoted to teaching classes of pupils predominantly aged nineteen and over, and they should spend the equivalent of at least ten school days teaching children of compulsory school age to demonstrate that they meet all the Induction Standards.

Schools that cannot provide induction include:

a   pupil referral units,
b   schools requiring special measures unless one of Her Majesty's Inspectors certifies in writing that the school is suitable for providing induction,
c   independent schools that do not teach the National Curriculum,
d   tertiary colleges, other than sixth form colleges.

Formal
assessment

Support and monitoring

Term
1

Setting of objectives for induction based on the CEP, school context and the induction standards

Observation of NQT and follow up discussion

Meeting to review progress and objectives

Week
5

Assessment meeting 1 with induction tutor and/or head teacher. Main focus: consistency in meeting standards for QTS.

Observation of NQT and follow up discussion

Meeting to review progress and objectives

Report sent by head teacher to Appropriate Body.

Individualised Support Programme for NQTs including, for example: observation of experienced teachers; discussion with school SENCO; where appropriate, training and advice from outside the school; taking part in external training events; participating in working groups.

Term
2

Observation of NQT and follow up discussion

Meeting to review progress and objectives

Assessment meeting 2 with induction tutor and/or head teacher. Main focus: progress in meeting induction standards.

Half
term

Observation of NQT and follow up discussion

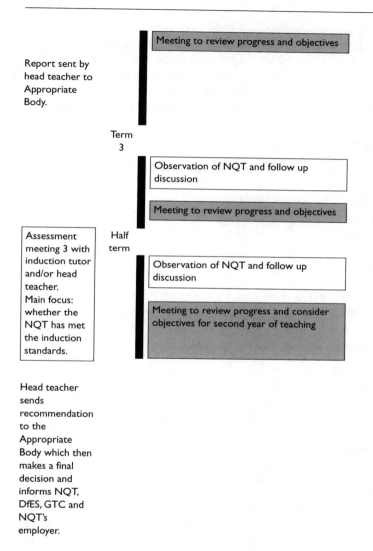

*Figure 1.1* Overview of the induction process (TTA 1999a: 6)

At the time of writing Jersey, Guernsey, the Isle of Man and Gibraltar follow England's induction regulations. However, teachers are not allowed to complete their induction year abroad, even if they are working in British schools. This is because there is no Appropriate Body for these schools.

These regulations only apply to England, Guernsey, Jersey, Gibraltar and the Isle of Man. Scotland has a two-year probation period, which is to be cut to one year in August 2002 and Northern Ireland has an induction stage in their teacher education programme. Induction in each country is recognised in England and vice versa. Wales does not yet have statutory induction arrangements but plans to introduce them in September 2003.

## How are NQTs assessed?

The requirements for the satisfactory completion of the induction year are two-fold:

1 By the end of the induction period NQTs should have consistently continued to meet the Standards for the award of Qualified Teacher Status.
2 They should also have met all the Induction Standards (DfEE 2000a).

There are ten Induction Standards. In order to meet them, the NQT should demonstrate that he or she does the following.

### Planning, teaching and class management

a Sets clear targets for improvement of pupils' achievement, monitors pupils' progress towards those targets and uses appropriate teaching strategies in the light of this, including, where appropriate, in relation to literacy, numeracy and other school targets;
b plans effectively to ensure that pupils have the opportunity to meet their potential, notwithstanding differences of race and gender, and taking into account the needs of pupils who are underachieving, very able, not yet fluent in English, making use of relevant information and specialist help where available;
c secures a good standard of pupil behaviour in the classroom through establishing appropriate rules and high expectations of discipline which pupils respect, acting to pre-empt and deal with inappropriate behaviour in the context of the behaviour policy of the school;
d plans effectively, where applicable, to meet the needs of pupils with Special Educational Needs and, in collaboration with the SENCO, makes an appropriate contribution to the preparation, implementation, monitoring and review of Individual Education Plans;
e takes account of ethnic and cultural diversity to enrich the curriculum and raise achievement.

### Monitoring, assessment, recording, reporting and accountability

f   Recognises the level that a pupil is achieving and makes accurate assessments, independently, against attainment targets, where applicable, and performance levels associated with other tests or qualifications relevant to the subject(s) or phase(s) taught;

g   liaises effectively with pupils' parents/carers through informative oral and written reports on pupils' progress and achievements, discussing appropriate targets, and encouraging them to support their children's learning, behaviour and progress.

### Other professional requirements

h   Where applicable, deploys support staff and other adults effectively in the classroom, involving them, where appropriate, in the planning and management of pupils' learning;

i   takes responsibility for implementing school policies and practices, including those dealing with bullying and racial harassment;

j   takes responsibility for their own professional development, setting objectives for improvements, and taking action to keep up to date with research and developments in pedagogy and in the subject(s) they teach.

## Our research

This book was inspired by the research project we carried out at the Institute of Education between September 2000 and December 2001 for the Department of Education and Skills (DfES). We evaluated the effectiveness of the mechanisms for carrying out induction of newly qualified teachers (NQTs), including the dissemination of information from central and local government. Most importantly we looked at the impact of induction on NQTs' classroom teaching and on the recruitment and retention of new teachers. We combined quantitative and qualitative research methods. For instance, we visited twenty-four schools of different sizes and types to carry out detailed case studies of how induction was working in specific contexts. We conducted semi-structured interviews with the NQTs, induction tutors and head teachers, visiting on two separate occasions in order to judge experiences at different stages in the induction year and the embedding of the policy over time.

This in-depth analysis of how the induction policy was working in schools substantiated the survey methods work – postal questionnaires to key players. We also conducted telephone semi-structured interviews with key personnel in local education authorities and supply teacher agencies.

We sent questionnaires to all England's 150 local education authorities (LEAs), a sample of head teachers and induction tutors in state schools throughout the country, and samples of the 1999–2000 and 2000–2001 cohorts of NQTs. We also wanted to find out how induction was going in non-standard settings, so we surveyed a selection of head teachers and induction tutors in independent schools, special schools and sixth form colleges (for students aged 16+). In total, there were over 220 interviews and over 1200 returned questionnaires, representing the views of NQTs, induction tutors, head teachers and LEA and supply teacher agency representatives.

We were keen to understand patterns of variability in induction provision in the context of the policy implementation process, and we became concerned with investigating what we termed the 'patchy periphery' where the full induction entitlements were not being received by NQTs. We also found much very good practice, and it is this that we wish to share in this book. First, here are our main findings.

## The main findings of our research project

Since the introduction of the statutory induction policy in September 1999, the quality of provision for newly qualified teachers has improved. There is overwhelming agreement among head teachers and induction tutors that statutory induction is helping NQTs to be more effective teachers.

The other main findings relate directly to the four research aims of the project.

### The effectiveness of mechanisms for carrying out the induction of NQTs

*The role of the school*

1   A large majority of respondents reported that the introduction of statutory induction had improved their school's induction provision. Almost all respondents who thought their school's induction provision had not improved said that they already had extensive induction programmes in place.
2   The number of NQTs on temporary contracts remains high, more than a third. No evidence, however, was found that those on temporary contracts receive lesser quality induction provision than those on full-time contracts.
3   Specific characteristics of certain schools often affect how induction is provided. In certain distinctive situations induction was usually more effective when managers paid appropriate consideration to alternative sources of personal support, particularly:

- in small schools, especially to overcome isolation when planning;
- in small schools where the head teacher has taken the role of induction tutor but has limited time to carry it out;
- in challenging schools (with multiple staffing shortages and challenging pupil behaviour);
- in areas where it is difficult to find satisfactory supply teachers to cover NQT release time.

4 The 10 per cent reduced teaching timetable is considered a vital component of induction provision by all involved. Despite this, our surveys of NQTs showed that 20 per cent of the 1999–2000 cohort and 19 per cent of the 2000–2001 cohort did not consistently receive this entitlement. Classroom release facilitates many other aspects of induction, such as attendance at training sessions and observations of other teachers, and so a significant minority of NQTs are experiencing less than full support.

5 The management of the use of release time is highly variable across schools. Between one-quarter and one-third of NQTs had no programme of activities; between one-third and a half had only occasional activities, and approximately one-quarter had a year-long programme.

6 Some head teachers and induction tutors expressed concern about NQTs who had to deal with particularly 'difficult' situations that were beyond their control. It was frequently suggested that these NQTs should be granted an extension and be moved to another school, to give them a better chance of success, rather than fail their induction period.

7 Whole school involvement in statutory induction is highly beneficial for NQTs. All staff need to be made aware of the school's induction provision and offered opportunities to contribute to NQTs' programmes of support and training.

8 Induction tutors in all types of school surveyed are predominantly senior teachers. Theirs is the key role in induction provision and they need to have a wide range of skills, knowledge and experience, including in-depth understanding of the standards for qualified teacher status and induction, and of the contexts of education and professional development. Many induction tutors are dedicated to maintaining good induction provision, often without being given time or financial reward.

9 The large majority of state school induction tutors received support and training for their role from the LEA, although a significant minority did not, which is a concern.

10 Observation and feedback *of*, and observation *by*, NQTs were found to be the most effective and cost-effective element of induction. The professional dialogue about teaching was particularly beneficial.

*The role of the Appropriate Body*

11  Appropriate Bodies are fulfilling their statutory role. A few are doing this to a minimum whilst many are going well beyond the statutory requirements in a variety of ways.

12  Of the support offered by Appropriate Bodies, networking and moderation sessions were considered most useful by induction tutors and NQTs alike. However, they were not universal and there were calls for more sessions of this type.

13  There was widespread consensus that a session introducing induction to NQTs, induction tutors and others in schools was essential and highly effective. Sessions on behaviour management were welcomed and appreciated, but other courses were seen to be less effective. Lack of opportunities to meet individuals' targets, repetition of material covered during initial teacher education and, most significantly, the organisation and presentation style of course leaders were heavily criticised.

14  Many NQTs said that certain entitlements were not consistently being provided by their schools. They made strong calls for their schools' induction provision to be monitored by Appropriate Bodies much more tightly than at present.

15  There is evidence to suggest that some schools and Appropriate Bodies are reluctant to fail NQTs because of the consequences of not being able to teach subsequently in the state-maintained sector. Rather, NQTs at potential risk of failing are encouraged to move to other schools which are not necessarily aware of their new teacher's background at the point of appointment.

16  Overall, schools reported that preparation and guidance received for induction from LEAs has improved. Training for induction tutors in assessing NQTs against the induction standards appears to have improved since the OFSTED findings in this area.

17  Quality assurance was systematically and thoroughly undertaken in some but by no means all Appropriate Bodies. For example, certain Appropriate Bodies gave no feedback to schools on assessment reports in ways that would assist future improvement. This issue raised serious concerns for maintaining the momentum of improvement.

*Cost effectiveness of the components of induction*

18  Funding arrangements vary within institutions but in all sectors surveyed the spending head/budget holder of the induction funds is a senior teacher or manager. In primary schools this is generally the head teacher (95 per cent).

19  The funding given to schools covers the NQTs' entitlement to a 90 per cent timetable, but leaves very little left over to cover other activities.

20 The LEA/Appropriate Body service agreement package can represent good value for money for schools, as they can include a range of elements, such as monitoring and assessment visits; support for induction tutors, and courses for NQTs. Given the high costs of releasing teachers from timetable, the provision in these service agreements is an important factor in the costs of induction to individual schools and colleges.

21 The most cost effective activity as viewed overall by all respondents is lesson observation of all kinds. This finding was reached by a correlation of sets of results: a variety of induction activities were rated for their *cost effectiveness* by head teachers, induction tutors and Appropriate Bodies. These activities were rated for their for *effectiveness as induction activities*, by NQTs. Head teachers/principals and Appropriate Body respondents said that lesson observations made *by* NQTs of other teachers teaching was the most cost effective activity, whereas induction tutors placed *'being observed'* and *'observing teachers in their own school'* almost equally highly. NQTs rated observing a teacher from their own school teach their own class as a very effective induction activity.

22 All meetings other than review and assessment meetings came next in ranked order, as most cost effective. The least cost effective induction activities are induction courses run by some private organisations or HEIs.

## The effectiveness of dissemination of information by DfES, TTA and Appropriate Bodies

23 Although most schools were aware of the new statutory induction standards, a proportion had not received relevant documentation, including the DfEE circular. In particular, information relating to assessment was found to be the least effectively disseminated information.

24 Numerous instances of confusion about induction were discovered. Some of these were lack of awareness of regulations, such as whether there is a time limit between gaining QTS and starting induction. Others were caused by their employing schools not meeting expectations based upon accurate interpretations of the regulations.

25 There is almost total confusion amongst supply teacher agencies about the definition and implications of the 'four term rule' for NQTs working on supply.

### The impact of induction on the effectiveness of NQTs' teaching and professional development

26  It is evident that the Career Entry Profile (CEP) is not working as intended. At best, the CEP acts as a summative judgement at the end of initial teacher education. Almost all targets written into CEPs at the end of initial teacher education courses were inappropriate in specific employment contexts. There is duplication within LEA, TTA and school professional development documents of the recording of targets, and there is little space in which to review them.

27  A large number of schools only review objectives at the end of each term, rather than half termly as is required by induction regulations.

28  NQTs are acutely aware of variability in different experienced staff's interpretations for assessment against the induction standards and differences of provision across schools and they are concerned that induction should be equitably implemented.

### The impact of induction on the recruitment and retention of NQTs

29  There was no evidence that certain groups (part-timers, temporary contracts, mature entrants, people from ethnic minorities, men or women) had received poor treatment in terms of induction provision.

30  The number of NQTs working as supply teachers has decreased radically. It seems from evidence that NQTs appreciate that being in a stable post is beneficial for a satisfactory completion of their induction period.

31  Head teachers, induction tutors and NQTs consider that induction is providing a bridge between initial teacher education and teaching. There is less evidence of it being so effective for the transition from the first year of teaching to further professional development, but this is thought to be more difficult for participants to judge. It was widely considered 'too early to tell' whether induction was having an impact on the recruitment and retention of NQTs through providing a 'bridge' between initial teacher education and further professional development.

32  Induction appears to be fitting in very well with the performance management in school. Head teachers and induction tutors found coherence between the two practices and expected future practical benefits.

# Chapter 2

# Why we have a statutory induction period

This chapter launches the rest of the book. It explains why induction for newly qualified teachers is so important. It outlines the ways in which previous induction policies were found to have failed and how it fits in with other current educational policies and issues.

The idea of induction is to formally introduce teachers to a post, an organisation (the school) and the teaching profession as a whole. The current statutory induction policy took effect on 7 May 1999. Our analysis of the relevant literature leads us to argue that it was introduced as a reaction to three main factors:

- the previous policy having not achieved what it intended,
- a substantial and persuasive body of research evidence which considers and highlights effective and less effective practices and procedures,
- the wider educational agenda of the current government.

## Previous induction policies

There have been many attempts to address induction, as can be seen in this list of key events in the history of induction policy:

- 1925 Board of Education attempts to link initial training and induction.
- 1944 McNair Report establishes the principle of assessing new teachers' work within a context of proper support.
- 1972 James Report seeks to establish appropriate balance between assessment and professional developments in the probationary year.
- 1982, 1987, 1993 HMI reports question the consistency of effective provision for new teachers.
- 1992 Probation was abolished by the Conservative Secretary of State Kenneth Clarke.
- Between 1992 and 1999 there were no national arrangements for NQTs.

- 1997 Career Entry Profile introduced to facilitate the transition between initial training and a teacher's first job.
- 1999 DFEE introduces the new statutory induction policy.

(Based on Simco 2000: 9)

Issues surrounding induction policy and practice have been stubbornly persistent over a long period of time. Much previous research highlighted the importance of good quality induction and the fact that it was not widely experienced. Between 1925 and 1972 there were three major attempts to move policy forward so that the first year of teaching had characteristics of both assessment and systematic professional development (Tickle 1994: 12; Simco 2000: 7–10). The rules concerning the probationary year as laid down in the Administration Memorandum 4/59 'Probation of Qualified Teachers', pp. 404–405, said this:

> 2.(a) The initial period of service of a teacher as a qualified teacher shall be a probationary period (which in the case of a full-time teacher who has satisfactorily completed a course of training specified in Schedule I shall be one year and in the case of any other teacher shall be two years) during which he may be required to satisfy the Secretary of State of his practical proficiency as a teacher, but in exceptional cases the Secretary of State may approve a probationary period which is less or more than one year (or as the case may be two years) or dispense with it entirely.
>
> (b) During his probationary period a teacher shall be employed in such a school and under such supervision and conditions of work as shall be suitable to a teacher on probation.
>
> (c) If at the end of the probationary period the Secretary of State determines the teacher to be unsuitable for further employment as a qualified teacher he shall not (without the approval of the Secretary of State) be so employed (and in the case of any teacher whose further employment is approved by the Secretary of State under this subparagraph the preceding provisions of this paragraph shall apply to the initial period of such further employment as if it were the initial period of his service as a qualified teacher).
>
> Schedule II (regulation 19)

The James Report of 1972 was important as it sought to provide proper support and monitoring of new teachers' work along with the assessment of their competence, in the expectation that there would be a more equal balance between assessment and professional development.

The three reports on induction by Her Majesty's Inspectors spanning the 1980s and early 1990s culminated in the publication of *The New Teacher in School*, written by Her Majesty's Inspectors (HMI 1993). This became highly influential with policy makers and practitioners and many aspects of the current statutory induction policy can be seen as stemming from this work. HMI found:

- most new primary teachers showed little awareness of a planned induction programme. Sixty-two per cent had no time formally allocated for induction in the school week.
- virtually all secondary schools ran induction programmes but their quality was variable. Three-quarters of new secondary teachers had a reduced teaching load, although this was rarely used for induction.
- there was little evidence that the planning of induction programmes was part of a systematic process of professional development beginning with initial training.
- induction was largely dependent on new teachers identifying their own needs. HMI considered that skills likely to require specific attention during induction included planning for differentiation, assessment of pupils' work and teaching pupils with special educational needs.
- new teachers considered that time spent on LEA induction programmes was not always well targeted. Individual visits of LEA staff to school, however, were appreciated.
- the quality of induction support for the weakest students working in difficult schools was unsatisfactory. Here, there were discrepancies between HMI's and the schools' assessment of weak teachers.
- about 10 per cent of the new teachers in the survey were considered ill-suited to teaching.

The HMI concluded that in 25 per cent of schools there were 'significant deficiencies in the capacity of the school to respond to the needs of new teachers' (HMI 1993: para. 5.14:36, adapted from Blake and Hill 1995: 317).

Probation was abolished in 1992 by the Conservative government, whose philosophy was that schools should be free to both organise and provide for their own staff, and that central government and LEAs should have little role to play. Research had consistently found that probation wasn't working consistently in practice. As a result of the abolition of probation, individual schools and LEAs were free to offer their own models of support – or none. For seven years, between 1992 and 1999, there was neither any assessment of the first year of teaching nor any requirement for schools to provide induction. It was simply up to the 'professional integrity of heads, teachers and advisers to sustain and encourage good practice' (Bleach 1999: 2). The concern was that, at worst, NQTs were left alone to 'sink or swim', and that the variability of provision that existed under probation would get worse.

Inconsistency in provision has been a long-running, central criticism of induction. The haphazardness meant the amount and quality of induction received was a matter of chance and depended on the school and LEA that a new teacher worked in. Induction provision was therefore seen as fundamentally unfair to NQTs and did not represent equal opportunities across the profession.

## No induction regulations 1992–1999

Between 1992 and 1999 some LEAs provided extensive induction programmes and training for mentors, bidding annually for funding from the TTA. Some worked with higher education institutions to accredit NQT and mentor training, and many produced and refined portfolios to aid NQTs' professional development. However, many LEAs found it hard to maintain induction support and programmes were cut. For instance, one London Borough, under the ILEA, was able to fund and organise a team of six induction coordinators working one day a week each. In that time they were able to run nine full-day courses for NQTs with supply cover paid to schools and give extensive training for mentors. They also visited each NQT several times a term. When probation was abolished and annual bidding rounds failed or diminished, the visits to NQTs in their schools were cut and the NQT induction course programme was reduced to twelve half days. This was a familiar story throughout the country.

In some schools, too, much good practice existed, and had done for a long time. Earley and Kinder (1994) described many places where exemplary work was going on. However, without the requirement to look after NQTs, some schools treated them badly, giving them only temporary contracts and no support. This variability of experience is summed up in Table 2.1, of NQTs' feelings about their schools' induction provision just before the introduction of the statutory regulations.

There were positive comments such as:

- 'Excellent support from mentor and all other members of staff, including non-teaching staff.'
- 'Mentor always available for advice. Staff very supportive. Non-contact time every week.'

*Table 2.1* NQTs' feelings about their school induction programme, July 1999 (Bubb 2000c: 2)

| How helpful was induction support in your school (%)? | | | | |
|---|---|---|---|---|
| Awful | Unsatisfactory | Satisfactory | Good | Very Good |
| 12 | 13 | 38 | 16 | 21 |

Negative comments, however, included statements such as these:

- 'Mentor chosen half a term after I began and she's only in her second year of teaching, didn't train in the UK, and hasn't got experience of teaching in my phase. The head never visits classrooms so there was no verbal or practical support from her. I still haven't been shown around the school! Policies are vague, schemes of work are vaguer!'
- 'School is in special measures and priorities are elsewhere, not on us. The pressure has been immense and support totally inadequate.'

So, in the years leading up to the introduction of statutory induction, there was a growing and widespread consensus (e.g. HMI 1993; Earley and Kinder 1994; Simco 1995; Mahoney 1996) that throughout the country:

- provision was highly variable,
- there were no systematic links between induction and the early professional development of teachers,
- the issue of individual needs was not uniformly addressed.

Bines and Boydell (1995), echoing the views of others, said 'effective induction should be systematic and planned, and be part of a school-wide approach to supporting staff roles and development, with all colleagues contributing to the general support, professional development and evaluation of NQT's progress' (p. 61).

Thus, in 1998 a consultation period started and on 7 May 1999 induction became statutory again.

## Induction as part of the educational reforms from 1997

Having a national policy for induction builds upon other recent education policies. For example, the introduction of partnerships between schools and teacher education institutions enabled some staff in the participating schools to be more confident about supporting, monitoring and assessing beginning teachers and using the competence-based assessment for qualified teacher status (Simco 2000: 13). The OFSTED inspection structure also meant that teaching and learning were discussed using common criteria, and led to more frequent, focused observations of teaching. The particular shape of teacher education reforms and the associated debates during the 1990s also went to shape both the overall concept or choice of definition and specific elements of post-September 1999 induction.

The statutory induction period was linked directly to the implementation of Threshold Assessment and Performance Management in 2000 and standards for qualified teacher status introduced in 1998. The close relationships between induction and other policies can be seen as significantly aiding the implementation of the new induction regulations. Indeed, they could be the key to its success after the disappointing results of previous induction policies.

Alongside the potentially positive context where induction is a coherent package with other professional and career development policies, are a number of concerns. The educational context of the years during which the induction regulations came into force (May 1999 onwards) was characterised by rapid policy implementation – some would say overload. Primary schools had worked very hard to implement the National Numeracy and Literacy Strategies and there followed other important initiatives:

- Curriculum 2000 – implemented September 2000,
- citizenship to be taught from September 2002 in secondary schools,
- curriculum guidance for the foundation stage – implemented September 2000,
- AS levels – implemented September 2000,
- Excellence in Cities, including the Gifted and Talented initiative,
- new SEN Code of Practice – due to begin September 2001, but delayed,
- Key Stage 3 literacy and numeracy strategy – implemented September 2001.

Thus, induction was but one significant initiative amongst many that LEAs and schools had to implement and plan for, while maintaining all other aspects of education. This raises questions about how well schools would implement the induction arrangements amongst everything else they had to do.

## Important themes within the policy of induction

There are a number of broad educational themes apparent in the overall intentions of the induction policy. The circular states that it has been introduced to provide:

- all newly qualified teachers with 'a bridge from initial teacher education to effective professional practice',
- 'a foundation for the ... long-term continuing professional development' of new teachers,
- 'well-targeted support ..., which in turn helps them to ... make a real and sustained contribution to school improvement and to raising classroom standards'.

(DfEE 2000a: para. 1)

So, there are three sets of reasons why the current government want a statutory induction policy and these link to its overall concerns in education, which are:

1 to raise standards of teaching and learning – in the classroom and for all, not just some, teachers,
2 to assist teacher recruitment and retention – by easing NQTs into the culture and work demands of the job,
3 to make a coherent path for the professional development of teachers.

## Induction and raising standards

There is no doubt that induction for NQTs is part of the current government's drive to raise teaching and learning standards. The 1997 Green Paper *Excellence in Schools* set the tone for the announcement of the reintroduction of statutory induction. It states:

> Teachers in a modern teaching profession need: to have high expectations of themselves and of all pupils; to take personal and collective responsibility for improving their skills and subject knowledge; to work in partnership with other staff in schools.
>
> (DfEE 1997: 2).

Induction is part of the 'unrelenting pressure on schools and teachers for improvement' and illustrates the aim to find the 'right balance of pressure and support which will enable us, together, to rise to the challenges of the new millennium' (ibid.: 11). Further, the government's policy-making principles include 'zero tolerance of underperformance', a focus 'on standards, not structures' and intend to 'benefit the many, not just the few'.

All these elements are present in the statutory induction policy. One of the government's principles is 'something for something' and balancing rights of support from government with responsibilities of individuals. In induction, the government is 'giving' support to NQTs in the form of a protected package of funded support and expects in return that school staff increase standards (Hextall and Mahony 1999: 15–16). The principle of 'zero tolerance of underperformance' is clearly demonstrated in the tough line that the regulations take on NQTs who do not meet the requirements for the end of the induction period: they are not allowed to teach in the maintained sector or non-maintained special schools again.

However, implementing these principles through induction is not always straightforward. For instance, one has to ask whether failing and barring people is fair. A *Times Educational Supplement* article tells of an NQT who failed after the first year that statutory induction was introduced. He says that he had 'to leave the profession permanently and acrimoniously' (Emmerson 2000) with no second chance. Pointedly, Bubb asks:

> Is a competence-based assessment that takes no account of individual contexts fair? ... Is it right that decisions about whether someone should pass or fail are taken by individual head teachers (with some input from Appropriate Bodies) and not by some national body, such as the General Teaching Council?
>
> (Bubb 2000b: 7)

Raising standards through better quality experiences in the first year of teaching is a laudable aim, but using induction as a way to weed out unsuccessful teachers leaves an unpleasant taste.

## Induction and teacher shortage

The *TES* had a record number of job vacancy adverts in the summer of 2001. At the end of August 2001 the Chief Inspector, Mike Tomlinson, said that teacher shortages were the worst since 1965 and that 40 per cent of teachers were leaving the profession before completing three years in the classroom (*TES* 28. 8.01: 1). A number of policies were introduced to encourage recruitment and retention. To help recruitment, from September 2000 training salaries were paid to trainee teachers on PGCEs (£6,000) and the Graduate Teacher Programme (£13,000). Golden Hellos (£4,000) were also given to those in shortage subjects. On 23 April 2001 legislation was passed allowing overseas-trained teachers to stay in the country for four rather than two years and to have an assessment-only route to gaining QTS with the option of being exempt from induction.

One of the intentions of induction is to help alleviate teacher shortage problems by encouraging those who hold QTS to enter and stay in the profession. Ralph Tabberer, the Chief Executive of the Teacher Training Agency speaking at the TTA/LGA conference in March 2000, said that induction would help to make the next generation of teachers 'the best, the best supported, the most positive, the most professional, the most enabled, the most enthusiastic' (Tabberer 2000). He went on to suggest, rather optimistically in light of the teacher shortage of the following year: 'Succeed and you achieve high retention and high recruitment' (Ibid. 2000). In theory, induction may encourage people to enter the profession – and not to leave it.

If induction contributes to teacher recruitment and retention figures then this is obviously useful for the profession as a whole. In the meantime, however, one has to ask how individual NQTs will fare in the current climate of teacher shortage. In schools where staffing levels are low, would they be able to be given a reduced timetable? Further, will the soaring number of places on the employment-based routes into teaching mean more work for school-based tutors; more classes taught by unqualified teachers, and so less experienced and accessible support for NQTs? There is also the possibility that having to complete a formally assessed induction period could deter more of those with QTS from entering the profession than it encourages in, via the entitlement to support that is offered.

## Induction as part of a professional development path

Induction is intended to be a bridge between training and the rest of a teacher's career. The latter is the focus of the Continuing Professional Development (CPD) Strategy. However, Tickle disagrees with the view that a continuum or bridge is necessary in the professional development of teachers, linking initial training, entry into full-time teaching and subsequent longer-term learning. He believes that NQTs should be prepared for 'discontinuities; radically new and different experiences; for turbulence ...' He thinks that the policy is predicated on a false picture of NQTs as deficient rather than seeing them as agents for change. NQTs are, he argues, 'an enviable resource' with 'creative potential' (Tickle 2000a: 11, 15).

Tickle is surely correct to point out that the assumption of an achievable continuity is questionable in that it fails to recognise adequately the inevitable turbulence that characterises the transition from initial training to induction. No amount of preparatory education and training can fully prepare NQTs for the challenges that they will face when they become teachers. The first year of teaching has always been difficult, as almost any serving teacher will testify. There are significant contextual differences between teaching as a student and as a 'real' teacher. But this fact must also qualify Tickle's ideal of new teachers as agents of change. Those whom Bolton calls the 'Pied Pipers of the Profession' (Bolton 1993: 3) may be able to affect change but this is not a realistic expectation of the majority of new teachers. It is probably better to recognise that there have long been tensions between the hopes and expectations of reform-minded teacher educators and the experiences of new teachers. Like any group, there will a wide range of effectiveness and, for some, induction will need to address deficiencies. However, all NQTs' potential teaching ability will surely be enhanced by long-term support that builds on their beliefs, knowledge and skills in a collaborative setting (Wideen et al. 1998).

All in all, the reasons why the induction policy was introduced seem coherent and the fact that there is funding should ensure that it is carried out effectively. However, our research found that though the policy has improved induction for many, some persistent problems remain. The implementation of the policy is complex – schools are complicated places and NQTs are very diverse, but the rest of this book offers numerous ways of how to maximise the chances of induction working well.

# Chapter 3

# How schools manage induction

This chapter describes how schools can manage statutory induction. We look at the importance of having a school policy and making clear the roles and responsibilities of head teachers, and other staff. The management of funding and employment contracts are also discussed. The key role of the induction tutor is explored in the following chapter.

## School induction policy

It is very important that schools have an induction policy, so that everyone knows about procedures, rights and responsibilities. The most effective policies we found were those in which there had been input from the people they affect, and which were regularly updated in the light of experience.

School policies should be based on an understanding of good practice, to ensure that procedures can be followed quickly, consistently and effectively by reference to agreed practices and principles (Bleach 2000). A school induction policy should serve to ensure that a structured induction programme is followed; everyone involved in induction are aware of their roles and responsibilities; individuals are aware of each other's roles and responsibilities, and NQTs are treated fairly and consistently. So a school policy on induction should cover three main areas:

- why the senior management team regards induction as beneficial for the school,
- the procedures staff should follow in order to support, monitor and assess NQTs,
- how NQTs can make best use of opportunities offered to them.

(Bleach 2000: 100)

Procedures that staff should follow can be outlined in induction policies through describing:

- the roles and responsibilities of individuals involved, including head teacher, induction tutor, induction manager if appropriate, other people involved in induction, the governing body, LEA staff,
- the induction programme which will be provided,
- guidance for assessment and monitoring of the NQT.

A procedure for review should also be included in the policy, to ensure that the school's intentions and procedures continue to be effective.

Below are examples of two schools' induction policies. It is interesting to see the differences in style as well as content. The first is addressed to the NQT, which defines the role and responsibilities of the school as a whole and of the new teacher (see Box 3.1). The second example (Box 3.2) defines the responsibilities of the school as a whole, though breaks this down slightly and describes the role of the head teacher/induction tutor and the LEA. It also states why the school is committed to providing the statutory induction provision.

## Head teachers

Head teachers have two key responsibilities:

1   to ensure that each NQT in their school is provided with an appropriate induction programme in line with national arrangements,
2   to make a recommendation to the LEA, based on rigorous and fair assessment procedures, as to whether or not the NQT has met the Induction Standards (TTA 1999a).

The head teacher can delegate many of the tasks associated with these responsibilities to the induction tutor or another suitably experienced colleague, but these two key responsibilities cannot be delegated. In order to meet these responsibilities, the head teacher should satisfy the guidelines outlined in Box 3.3 by the TTA (TTA 1999a).

Tasks which the head teacher can delegate, while retaining overall responsibility, are shown in Box 3.4.

## Organisation in schools

Schools need to share specific induction responsibilities between the head teacher and induction tutor, and other staff may be allocated roles. Earley and Kinder (1994) found in the early 1990s that there were induction systems that they called:

- mono-support,
- tri-support,
- bi-support,
- multi-support.

**Your induction year: who does what and when in the first term**

**The school will:**

By the end of the first month:

- negotiate an agreed Individual Action Plan with you, identifying objectives for professional development for the first term (Section C of the Career Entry Profile).
- ensure that the induction tutor observes you.
- provide an appropriate weekly support programme for you.

During the term:

- ensure that the induction tutor maintains a written record of all support, monitoring and assessment evidence carried out in relation to your progress.
- ensure that half-termly review sessions take place between your induction tutor and you.

By the end of the term:

- ensure that the induction tutor carries out a formal assessment of your progress according to national guidelines and criteria.
- ensure that the induction tutor conducts the first formal assessment meeting with you, providing well-founded feedback on your progress.
- return the appropriate Record of Assessment to the LEA induction team.

**You will:**

By the end of the first month:

- negotiate an agreed Individual Action Plan with the induction tutor.
- attend the weekly NQT meeting (Tuesdays, 3.30pm–4.30pm).

During the remainder of the term:

- develop your professional practice to meet the objectives agreed in your Individual Action Plan.
- respond to feedback from lesson observations.
- keep a written record of all support, monitoring and assessment carried out by the college.
- meet each half term with your induction tutor to review progress.
- attend the first LEA conference for NQTs.

*continued*

Box 3.1 Induction policy for term one (secondary)

**Aims and Objectives**

- To enable the NQT to become an effective teacher.
- To encourage and promote the confidence of the NQT.
- To enable the NQT to become a good classroom practitioner.
- To ensure that the NQT feels welcome and is made to feel a valuable member of the school community.

**Responsibilities of the school**

- To find a suitable placement taking into consideration the Career Entry Profile, curriculum strengths and the interest of the NQT.
- To provide a programme of induction pre and post appointment, both within the context of the school and that offered by the LEA.
- To offer support through the appointment of an experienced teacher induction tutor to the NQT.
- To familiarise the NQT with the policies of the school, offering guidance regarding their implementation.
- To inform the NQT of procedures which operate within the school.
- To inform the NQT of staff responsibilities, in the context of curriculum, age groups, ethos and management.
- To offer opportunities to observe other classes and examples of good practice, and to visit other schools.
- To provide guidance with the planning and delivery of the curriculum.
- To provide suggestions regarding classroom organisation and discipline.
- To hold regular meetings and provide opportunities for informal feedback.
- To encourage continuous self-evaluation, review and development.
- To monitor the progress made by the NQT and set appropriate targets for future development, and ensure the NQT meets the induction standards.

**The head teacher/induction tutor**

- Will observe the NQT teaching and provide verbal and written feedback.
- Periodically review, with the NQT, the children's work.
- Periodically review, with the NQT, any record keeping and forecasts.
- The head teacher will regularly discuss progress through meetings with the induction tutor.
- Alert all staff to the role they can play in supporting and encouraging the NQT.
- Provide praise, support and encouragement.
- Liaise with the adviser.

**Responsibilities of the LEA**

- The LEA will offer a series of induction meetings to familiarise NQTs with LEA policy and personnel.
- A programme of courses may be arranged addressing specific needs identified by NQTs.
- Provide initial training for induction tutors.
- Give guidance to the school from school improvement officers as and when necessary.
- Give opportunities for NQTs to share problems, experience and ideas with others and their induction tutors.
- Provide an induction programme to deal with specific topics, e.g. classroom management, equal opportunities, safety and areas of the curriculum identified by NQTs.
- Give information about support provided by the LEA.
- Provide the opportunity to take part in a residential weekend with a structured programme of activities.

*Box 3.2* Induction policy (primary)

- Designate an induction tutor for each NQT, and ensure that this person is adequately prepared and is able to work effectively in the role. In some cases, head teachers may wish to designate themselves as induction tutors.
- Make sure that any duties assigned to the NQT are reasonable.
- Make sure that the NQT is provided with a timetable representing no more than 90 per cent of the average contact time normally allocated to more experienced teachers in the school, and make sure that the time released is protected, is distributed appropriately throughout the induction period and is used to support the NQT's professional development right from the start of the induction period.
- Provide the NQT with a way of raising concerns about the induction programme, and make sure that these concerns are addressed satisfactorily.
- Inform the LEA about any NQT who may be at risk of failing to meet the induction standards and observe the teaching of the NQT concerned.
- Keep the Governing Body informed about arrangements for the induction of NQTs in the school, and the results of formal assessment meetings.

(TTA 1999a)

*Box 3.3* TTA guidelines on head teacher responsibilities

- Devising, together with the NQT, a targeted and appropriate monitoring, support and assessment programme, building on the Career Entry Profile and drawing on external resources where relevant.
- Making arrangements for any additional experience that the NQT may need to gain in settings outside the school (for example, in a nursery or post-16 setting) or for further support that needs to be provided by specialists (for example, for an NQT teaching a minority subject).
- Telling the LEA when any teacher who is subject to the induction arrangements either joins or leaves the school.
- Sending the LEA the reports completed after formal assessment meetings.
- Liaising with other head teachers and LEAs as appropriate in relation to NQTs employed on a part-time basis in more than one school at the same time.
- Making sure that any relevant reports and records are obtained from any school(s) in which an NQT has served part of their induction, and forwarding copies of any previously completed assessment reports to the LEA.
- Making sure that copies of all reports of observations, review meetings and objectives are kept until the induction period has been completed satisfactorily and any appeal determined.
- Keeping copies of any records or assessment reports for those NQTs who leave the school before completing the induction period, and forwarding these to the NQT's new school when requested, submitting the relevant assessment form, taken from Annex B in the Guidance to the Appropriate Body within ten working days of completion of the induction period.

(TTA 1999a)

Box 3.4 Tasks which head teacher may delegate

Schools in our research organised induction personnel in a similar range of ways, as Figure 3.5 shows.

One might imagine that the more people an NQT gets support from the better, and indeed we found instances where people benefited from getting help from a range of colleagues. However, we found several instances where NQTs suffered as a result of responsibility being shared. For instance an NQT in a secondary school with two levels of support suffered because the heads of departments did not do their job properly (observing every half term, setting and reviewing targets and having regular meetings). It was only at the end of term that the induction coordinator realised this, however.

**Primary School 1 (mono-support)**
Induction tutor:             Member of the senior management team

**Primary School 2 (mono-support)**
Induction tutor             Head teacher

**Primary School 3 (bi-support)**
Induction tutor             Member of the senior management team
Mentor             The parallel class teacher

**Primary School 4 (tri-support)**
Induction coordinator:  Member of the senior management team
Induction tutor:           Year group leader
Buddy mentor:         A recently qualified teacher

**Secondary School 1 (mono-support)**
Induction tutor             Senior member of staff

**Secondary School 2 (bi-support)**
Induction coordinator:  Senior member of staff in charge of all NQTs in the school
Induction tutor:           The head of department

**Secondary School 3 (tri-support)**
Induction coordinator:  Senior member of staff in charge of all NQTs in the school
Induction tutor:           The head of department
Buddy mentor:         A recently qualified teacher

**Secondary School 4 (tri-support)**
Induction tutor/ coordinator:  A senior teacher who organises the induction programme, meetings, assessment reports, etc.
Academic mentor:     The head of department who advises on all subject related matters
Pastoral mentor:     A head of year who gives guidance on behaviour management and pastoral issues

**Secondary School 5 (multi-support)**
Staff Development Officer:  In charge of coordinating the induction programme for all NQTs and organises contracts, job descriptions, staff handbook and the pre-induction visits before the NQTs start work
Subject mentor:      Head of the department that the NQT works in: supervises planning and teaching and gives subject specific input
Pastoral mentor:     A head of year who gives guidance on behaviour management and pastoral issues
Buddy mentor group:  A group of recently qualified teachers who provide a shoulder to cry on

*Box 3.5* Organisation of induction personnel

On the other hand, sharing responsibility means that the induction tutor's considerable workload is lessened. Shared responsibility worked best in schools with good communication systems.

## Monitoring

Induction tutors are responsible for the day-to-day support, monitoring and assessment of NQTs but the head teacher, along with the Appropriate Body, is responsible for ensuring that each NQT has an appropriate induction programme and for monitoring its quality (DfEE 2000a: para. 15). This includes making sure that the induction period provides a programme of monitoring and support which addresses individual NQT's needs and helps them to meet the requirements of the induction period (DfEE 2000a: para. 39). However, our research found inconsistency in the quality of induction arrangements between NQTs in the same school (OFSTED 1999). Thus, monitoring of induction provision is important in order to prevent inequality.

Head teachers may delegate induction provision to the induction tutor, but they themselves should monitor this provision. Ideally the monitoring of induction provision should include communication between the head teacher and all parties involved in order to gain a range of perspectives. Monitoring should be an ongoing process to ensure that the induction provision is satisfactory throughout the year. At the beginning of the induction year monitoring may occur through:

- a meeting with all relevant parties, including the NQT, to discuss the allocation of resources to the NQT,
- monitoring the establishment of the NQT's workload and timetable to ensure they are not unreasonable.

In our research we found that monitoring was rather haphazard. It should continue throughout the year with head teachers maintaining an overview of induction provision. This can be done through communication, both verbal and written, with the induction tutor and a discussion of provision with the NQT.

If head teachers find their role in monitoring hard to fulfil they can identify external sources of help such as LEA advisers or educational consultants. The two case studies below demonstrate how schools use external support.

**Case study**

A head teacher in a small rural school found monitoring difficult. This was because he had a 70 per cent teaching timetable and so had very little time available for induction. Therefore he sought help from outside the school and bought in LEA advisers to help.

**Case study**

A large inner-city comprehensive with many problems including staffing shortages bought in an educational consultant. She visited once a month to give the three NQTs intensive support. She monitored their progress, carried out observations, and tried to meet the common training needs of the group. She fed back to the induction tutor, who was responsible for completing the assessment forms.

## Governors

The school governing body has three key responsibilities:

- when appointing new staff to take into account the school's responsibility to provide the necessary monitoring, support and assessment for NQTs,
- to oversee the establishment and implementation of induction arrangements,
- to seek guidance, if it wishes, from the LEA on induction arrangements and the roles of those school staff with responsibility for implementing them.

(DfEE 2000a: para. 33)

The TTA describes how governors may 'wish to think about their responsibilities for induction in the context of both their wider role in the quality assurance of teaching and learning in the school and their role in staff employment matters' (TTA 1999d: 7).

Head teachers should keep the governing body informed of arrangements for induction provision and the results of NQTs' formal assessment meetings (DfEE 2000a: para. 16). We found that governors were generally informed through head teachers' termly/yearly reports or staffing committee reports. Some head teachers in our research said that had the induction provision not been satisfactorily implemented then the governors would have become more involved.

Some of the staff we interviewed thought that it would be beneficial for governors to play a greater role and be more involved with NQTs and induction. Schools can do this in a range of ways:

- a particular governor is assigned as a 'link induction' governor,
- governors meet NQTs at the beginning of the induction year,
- governors help evaluate individual NQT's induction provision.

The following case studies demonstrate how governors can be involved with induction.

**Case study**

In one primary school the link governor had met with the NQT before the start of the statutory induction year. This meeting was used to introduce the NQT to the school and to discuss what the NQT expected from the school. The governor then fed this information back to the induction tutor and deputy head teacher.

**Case study**

A secondary school nominated one of its governors as the person with whom the NQT should raise any concerns within the school. This governor was given the title of 'induction governor'. The induction governor held an evaluation meeting in the spring term and interviewed all staff involved with induction provision, including the NQTs, to ensure that the process was progressing smoothly.

## Funding

One of the greatest facets of statutory induction is the earmarked funding that can enable it to happen. The DfES allocated £64.4m specifically for induction for NQTs in 2001–2002. However, there have been snags in the way funding is organised, only some of which have been ironed out.

When induction first became statutory (1999 to 2000) schools were given money for induction through Grant 1 of the Standards Fund. However, this grant covered many areas related to school effectiveness including improving standards of pupil performance to meet school, LEA and national targets; securing urgent improvement in schools causing concern; implementing new appraisal arrangements from September 1999 and funding LEA central support for school improvement activities. Consequently, there were wide variations in induction funding:

- the NUT found that funding in the autumn term 1999 ranged from £450 to £1,200 per NQT per term,
- OFSTED found the amount allocated by different LEAs for the period from September 1999 to Easter 2000 varied from £335 to £2,533 per NQT and in the summer term of 2000 it varied from £350 to £1,509 (OFSTED 2001c: para. 283),
- our research found that 42 per cent of head teachers were unable to say how much money their school received for induction. Of those who could tell us, the amounts varied considerably, with 7 per cent saying that they received no money.

As a result of this inequality, the Standards Fund arrangements were altered for 2001–2002 (DfEE 2001) so that induction had its own category (category 501 in the 2001–2002 arrangements). Since April 2001, LEAs have been required to ensure that each school receives no less than £1,000 per term for each of the summer, autumn and spring terms for each NQT, including those undergoing induction who are employed by supply agencies. This amount is the same for schools throughout the country with no allowance made for areas such as London where supply teachers are more expensive than in other areas. This continues to be a pressing equal opportunity issue as it disadvantages NQTs in certain schools.

However, schools which have City Technology College (CTC) status are not assigned a specific sum of money to be used for induction provision, because their funding is organised differently to other schools (correct at the time of publication). This resulted in some NQTs having difficulty in getting their 10 per cent reduced timetable. Therefore, it may be even harder to ensure that the full entitlement of provision is received by all NQTs.

Sixth Form Colleges receive £1,175 per NQT per term as opposed to £1,000 in other maintained schools (correct at the time of publication). This is due to the colleges having to pay the LEA approximately £175 to provide the Appropriate Body service.

### What the funding will pay for

The £1,000 funding per term per NQT has clearly helped schools to implement statutory induction. However, the FEFC research into sixth form colleges found that 'most colleges found that their expenditure exceeded the income from the standards fund' (FEFC 2001: para. 38). Release time for all teachers involved in induction often involves cover costs. At the time of our research, supply agencies charged between £120–£180 depending on the geographical area. The inner cities cost more than other areas. Costs are also rising rapidly because of teacher shortages.

We calculated the spending power of the £1,000 per term per NQT, taking the 10 per cent release time into account. This time has to be costed, either to pay for supply or to transfer into the staffing budget, where the NQT has designated, timetabled non-contact time. Our calculations showed that the 10 per cent release time is covered by the funding, but very little is left over, as the following suggests.

Additional employer costs to salaries are usually calculated at 16 per cent. Thus, real salary costs of an NQT vary between £18,604 p.a. and £26,680 p.a. This is calculated at one end of the scale (at April 2001) for an NQT on the starting salary of £16,038 p.a. with no points for previous experience or recruitment and retention, and no local allowances. The other end of the scale represents a good honours graduate starting at £17,001 p.a. with 2 points for recruitment and retention, which are paid by some schools particularly in areas with staffing shortages. Some NQTs also gain points for previous experience and there may be local allowances, such as the £3,000 London weighting.

Replacing 10 per cent of this time can cost a school between approximately £1,860 p.a. and £2,660 p.a. This leaves a variable sum for all the other elements of an induction programme. In some schools there may be as little as £300 left over, whereas in other schools there may be much more.

Another method of calculation is to consider the costs of supply cover. The daily rate for a supply teacher during our research was between £120–£180 per day, so calculating the school year as 38 weeks, the cost of giving 10 per cent release time would be between £2,280 p.a. and £3,420 p.a.

The induction tutor's time does not appear in this calculation. As mentioned above, the school absorbs these costs if time is made available, or by the induction tutor if no non-contact time is available.

Thus, the £1,000 per NQT per term can fund release time but there is little left over for other elements of the training and support programme. Costs for the 10 per cent release time are significantly higher in some areas than in others, but this is not reflected in the funding of £1,000 per term for all.

### Additional costs

Schools have to meet additional costs, whether from the induction funding or other budgets. These costs are listed below and include their price, correct at the time of publication.

- LEA/AB service agreement package: which schools can buy into from around £150 to £450 and can include a range of elements, such as monitoring and assessment visits, support for induction tutors, courses for NQTs. Some schools do not pay at all for these services.

- Courses cost in the range £70–£200 per day, plus travel expenses.
- Release time for induction tutors and other staff to carry out lesson observations of NQTs, and to hold meetings, including those for review and assessment. These elements are hard to cost given that the time of induction personnel is given when required, and not strictly calculated on an hourly basis. Our evidence suggests that time is given well over and above the time that the funding releases. A key recommendation from our research is that there should be ear-marked funding for induction tutors to enable them to do the job.

Some schools consider their greatest resource to be their own staff and consequently they are happy to use money from other budgets to release teachers to support NQTs. They see it as a wise investment.

**Case study**
The head teacher of a primary school used the funding for induction of the school's three NQTs to release the induction tutor from her classroom teaching two days a week. This induction tutor was then available to cover the NQTs' classes and to conduct lesson observations, meetings and monitoring. As much of the induction budget was used for the induction tutor's release, induction activities were supplemented from other budgets under headings such as 'school improvement' and 'raising achievement'. Both the head teacher and the induction tutor thought the money from these other budgets was well spent. The head teacher felt that the budget was secondary to the quality of input for NQTs and saw their arrangement as cost-effective.

## Contracts

### Part-time

In both 1999–2000 and 2000–2001, around 10 per cent of NQTs in our research were on part-time contracts. This group are potentially difficult for schools to manage since they have to work out what their entitlement is pro rata. The induction period for a part-time NQT is calculated pro rata so that the same number of school sessions is covered as for a full-time NQT (DfEE 2000a: para. 34). For example, if an NQT worked 50 per cent of a school's normal hours, then the induction period would last six school terms, or two years.

Part-time NQTs have to have a 10 per cent reduced teaching timetable. This should be calculated as 10 per cent of their part-time timetable, which can be hard to organise if the NQT is only working one or two days a week. It is most useful if it can be blocked into half-day sessions to enable the teacher to visit other classrooms. The reduced timetable is as essential for a part-time NQT as it is for one who teaches full time.

The intervals between a part-time NQT's observations should be adjusted accordingly but the first observation should take place in the first half term (DfEE 2000a: para. 47). A full-time NQT should be observed at least once in any six to eight week period, usually once every half term. Therefore, part-time NQTs working 50 per cent of a school's normal hours should be observed at least once in any twelve to sixteen week period, so once a term.

Where an NQT is employed part-time in more than one school at the same time, only one head teacher and Appropriate Body can be responsible for an NQT and the head teachers should agree which of them should take on the respective responsibilities (DfEE 2000a: para. 18). However, it is important that both schools support the NQT.

### Temporary

In our research around 35 per cent of NQTs in state schools were on temporary contracts, for the academic years of 1999–2000 and 2000–2001, with slightly more in secondary than primary schools. This is clearly a higher percentage than one would expect, and is thus very worrying.

Teachers on temporary contracts have to deal with greater job insecurity, inequality and lower status, which can be de-motivating for NQTs. Issuing an NQT a temporary contract goes against the principle of the induction year acting as a bridge from training into teaching as a career. Therefore temporary contracts should only be used where the period of employment is not known as the NQT is covering maternity or sick leave. It is unacceptable to use such contracts as a form of probation for the NQT. Many schools hold a policy of giving temporary contracts and then reviewing NQTs after a year to see if they 'make the grade'. Appropriate Bodies we spoke to said that they encouraged schools not to employ NQTs on temporary contracts as the induction period meant this was not necessary. However, four LEAs we spoke to had between 39 per cent and 58 per cent of NQTs on temporary contracts.

The induction provision for NQTs on temporary contracts should be the same as full-time NQTs on permanent contracts. If teachers who are on a temporary contract stay at a school for a term, it will count towards the induction year. Head teachers and induction tutors should send a completed assessment form to the Appropriate Body at the end of the term. If the teacher has not made satisfactory progress they will still have served a full term's induction and will need to be supported in another school, in order to 'make the grade' by the end of the next two terms.

### Non-September starter

Although most NQTs start their induction in September, some start later. This can cause difficulties for schools.

Around a quarter of state schools and sixth form colleges we surveyed had taken on NQTs from another school during their induction, whilst in independent and special schools this figure was around 10 per cent. Most NQTs who moved into the schools in this survey did so at some point during the spring term. Interestingly, more state secondary schools had non-September starters than primary schools, possibly due to teacher shortages in secondary schools.

An NQT joining a new school having completed part of the induction period in another school may require some additional introductory support, especially if time has passed between these periods of service (DfEE 2000a: Annex C).

Most state head teachers surveyed in our research thought that employing non-September starters had not made a difference to the induction provision the school normally provided. Head teachers said the extent to which their induction provision had altered was highly dependent on the previous position and experience of the NQTs employed. Those that thought it had made a difference to their provision described how their NQTs had come from a different LEA/school which did not provide or had inadequately covered parts of the statutory induction programme. Consequently, such respondents described how they had to perform various 'rescue programmes' and 'initial needs assessments'. It may also mean that relevant induction courses are sometimes missed, which may have to be detailed to the new NQT on a one-to-one basis. In order to avoid such problems, when NQTs move between schools information should move with them, as in the case study below.

**Case study**

A secondary school employed an NQT who started after September. The NQT had previously been employed in a school in the same LEA as his new school. The NQT's previous school had provided good information regarding the NQT's induction programme followed, and assessment documentation. This had meant that the NQT's transition between schools was smooth and he was able to continue with induction effectively.

Communication between schools is very important in order to maintain consistency in the NQT's induction. If an NQT leaves a school before completing induction the head teacher should retain any records or summative assessment reports and forward these to the NQT's new school when requested (DfEE 2000a: para. 18). It is then the responsibility of the head teacher who receives the NQT to ensure that any relevant reports and records are obtained from the previous school.

**Case study**
An NQT moved schools during her second term of induction. The NQT said that her new induction tutor had made an effort to find out what her induction provision had been like in the previous school. This included the new school requesting relevant documentation from the previous school, including the induction programme and any assessment records. The NQT explained that as a result she felt that she did not have to start the induction process all over again.

## Whole school impact

Induction may benefit schools through contributing to:

- the development of a school's involvement in initial teacher training,
- the establishment of an effective system for continuing professional development: which begins in the statutory induction year and continues into subsequent years of teaching,
- the development of a strong recruitment and retention strategy: for example through offering a supportive induction package.

The TTA also describe how, if induction tutors are well supported and successful in their role, schools may see improvements in:

- teaching and learning: by encouraging teachers to engage in focused discussions, planning and designing collaboratively, observing and reviewing teaching,
- ability to monitor and evaluate standards: through induction tutors' experience of using a range of evidence,
- performance management arrangements for second-year teachers: who will move smoothly into the performance management cycle with objectives from the end of their first year's teaching,
- performance management arrangements more widely: through induction tutors' experience of negotiating, setting and reviewing

professional development objectives and arranging subsequent support,
- NQT induction in subsequent years,
- the school's involvement in initial teacher training: including employment-based routes into teaching,
- the ability of induction tutor to contribute to the planning and provision of support for teachers in the second and third years of teaching: with a potential impact on the retention of effective teachers in the school,
- the ability of induction tutors to contribute to planning for school improvement: for instance, post-OFSTED action planning.

(TTA 2001b: 9)

# Chapter 4

# Induction in distinctive settings

All NQTs have the same full entitlement to induction, such as the 10 per cent release time, a suitably experienced induction tutor and a programme of support, monitoring and assessment. However, certain groups of school, college and NQT require particular consideration when providing induction. This chapter covers five 'settings' which our research evidence found to be distinctive in terms of specific requirements for effective induction. These are:

- sixth form colleges,
- independent schools,
- special schools,
- small schools,
- supply teachers.

The experience of undergoing and providing induction in one of these five settings was not found to be any worse or better than in other mainstream state schools.

## Sixth form colleges

NQTs were not initially allowed to undergo statutory induction in a sixth form college. It was only after pressure that legislation was passed making it a possibility. Thus, NQTs in these colleges have only been able to do statutory induction since September 2000. By and large induction is the same for NQTs in sixth form colleges as it is in schools. They have the same entitlement to a 10 per cent reduced timetable, an induction tutor, and observations, and the other requirements. However, there are significant differences.

1  Statutory induction is optional for NQTs in sixth form colleges. Sixth form colleges do not have to offer it and even if they do, NQTs can choose not to undergo induction in this context – a choice that is not possible in a school.

2   It can only be offered to NQTs who hold Qualified Teacher Status (QTS). Some will have taken a PGCE in post-compulsory education which only qualifies them to teach students over the age of 16. They do not have QTS.

3   No more than 10 per cent of an NQT's teaching should be devoted to teaching classes of students predominantly aged nineteen and over.

4   NQTs should spend the equivalent of at least ten days teaching students of compulsory school age. This is to enable all the induction standards to be met.

5   Induction tutors in sixth form colleges must have QTS. (Some teachers may not have QTS, if they have a PGCE in post-compulsory education.)

6   Colleges have to have an Appropriate Body, but need not choose their local LEA.

Sixth form colleges organise cover to provide the 10 per cent release time for NQTs differently to schools. Supply teachers are rarely used. Many induction activities are organised when examinations are taking place.

In general, we found that statutory induction has had quite a strong impact on NQTs in sixth form colleges. For example, three-quarters of sixth form induction tutors thought that statutory induction had helped NQTs' professional continuity and progression, from initial teacher training into teaching, to a substantial extent. The vast majority of sixth form colleges also said that statutory induction has improved the preparation,

---

- Appropriate Bodies appeared to be less actively involved in induction in sixth form colleges than in schools. Only half of the induction tutors had attended one or more training or networking session.
- NQTs and induction tutors were dissatisfied with many induction courses because of the school-focused content.
- A few small groups of sixth form colleges negotiate joint Service Level Agreements with LEAs for support, monitoring and assessment. They buy these services at a lower cost than could be done individually.
- Only just over half of sixth form colleges received key induction documents. They found the DfES circular and the TTA's *Supporting Induction* booklets useful but wanted material specifically for sixth form colleges.
- Sixth form college induction tutors find the Career Entry Profile to be of very limited use, because the strengths and areas for development that NQTs identify at the end of their training in schools are rarely relevant to the sixth form college context.

---

*Box 4.1* Summary of our findings for induction in sixth form colleges

support and assessment that their institution provides. However, the degree of improvement had been less than, for example, independent schools, because extensive induction programmes were usually already in place.

### The secondary school placement

The requirement for sixth form college NQTs to do a placement in a school was brought in to provide the opportunity to meet all the induction standards and so that subsequent posts could be more easily taken up in schools. In practice, however, the school placement is considered highly problematic by most sixth form colleges. One induction tutor told us what they thought would improve induction:

> Remove the requirement for 2 weeks 11–16 experience for those completing induction in a sixth form college. It is too brief to be of real use and the college would prefer to have them teaching here!

Another spoke of the 'huge additional burden' the organisation of the placement creates for induction coordinators. Subjects did not necessarily match where for instance an NQT taught psychology in the sixth form college. It is also considered disruptive for students' course work, both at the school and college.

NQTs dislike the placement too. They feel undervalued, considering it to be a retrograde step, like being on teaching practice again. They see little benefit to it – just a hoop to jump through. It causes problems of additional workload. For instance, we found instances where NQTs were not only having to prepare lessons to teach in their school placement but also having to leave work for their sixth form students to do in their absence.

In the light of this evidence it is understandable that feelings about the secondary school placement run high. It is also considered unfair. Some asked why NQTs in sixth forms should have to do school placements when, for example, NQTs in nursery schools do not have to do primary school placements? Our findings corroborate those of the Further Education Funding Council's induction research report (FEFC 2001).

### Improving induction in sixth form colleges

At present, there is little that sixth form colleges can do to avoid the statutory requirement of placing their NQTs in schools for ten days or more. However, there are ways to improve the situation:

- induction co-ordinators could ask their Appropriate Body to help establish permanent arrangements with schools that do not need re-negotiating each year and for each subject.

- adopt the practice of several colleges and make the school placement coincide with exam periods. There will be fewer classes needing cover.
- continue to assert that this requirement is unfair.

Support received from Appropriate Bodies is not always tailored to their particular needs. There are several ways that colleges can work with Appropriate Bodies to receive suitable support. At present the DfES and TTA documents are oriented towards schools and no induction standards are written specifically for sixth form students. The experience of one induction tutor led him to identify three needs from Appropriate Bodies:

- production of post-16-specific induction documentation,
- help in fostering dedicated links with 11–16 schools for an NQT's placement,
- provision of relevant and cost-effective support.

**Case Study: Richard**

Richard volunteered to be an induction tutor but had little prior experience of this type of work. He told us:

> I received virtually nothing in the way of support and preparation at the beginning except for a mound of paperwork. Training courses which explain how to interpret the paperwork in practice would be very helpful. Support networks are needed. Local groups need setting up. They could link up induction tutors for both mutual support and organisation of 'exchanges' of NQTs so they can do observations in each other's schools.

## Independent schools

NQTs do not have to pass induction in order to teach in an independent school. Nevertheless, a very large number of NQTs in independent schools are doing their induction period. This gives teachers the option to move into the state sector later in their career and provides a structured course of professional training.

Like sixth form colleges, independent schools can choose whether or not to offer statutory induction to their NQTs. They can only do so if the school teaches the National Curriculum to any primary aged pupils for which it has responsibility. Independent schools also need an Appropriate Body, but they have the option of using either an LEA or a body called ISCTIP – the Independent Schools Council Teacher Induction Panel. Only schools that belong to one of the five professional bodies affiliated to the

Independent Schools Council (ISC) can use ISCTIP. Others would have no option but to ask an LEA to be their Appropriate Body. Some LEAs evaluate the quality of education offered by a school before agreeing to act as the Appropriate Body, whereas other LEAs accept all who approach them, without any quality control procedures.

Once it has been formally agreed between a head teacher, NQT and Appropriate Body that induction will be provided, all the statutory elements must be provided and completed in full. There has been some confusion caused by head teachers apparently saying to NQTs that they will provide induction but then not following the full statutory model. Further, government funding (£1,000 per term per NQT) is not available to independent schools. They therefore pay for support, monitoring and assessment out of their own school budgets.

---

1　Independent schools had considerably less interaction with their Appropriate Bodies than state schools. Only 45 per cent of induction tutors attended training. The one-day conference run by ISCTIP was highly praised by those who have attended it. LEAs were rated a little more effective than ISCTIP when it came to providing information about training and courses on offer. ISCTIP visited 25 per cent of schools with NQTs doing induction, to support and monitor the provision. LEAs varied in the number and frequency of visits to schools depending on the prior agreement reached between them and a Principal.

2　None of the independent schools receive funding from external sources. Rather, general school funds are used.

3　Only one-third of independent schools received all three key induction documents – the DfEE circular, TTA *Supporting Induction* booklets and Appropriate Body packs. Correspondingly, one-third found that dissemination of information had not been very effective.

4　One-third of induction tutors in independent schools are deputy head teachers. One-third were given release time for this role, which is quite high.

5　Only 2 per cent of induction tutors in all independent schools surveyed received extra salary points for the role. In state schools it was 13 per cent.

6　Every one of the induction tutors surveyed had previously been professional tutors for students on initial teacher education courses and 28 per cent were responsible for NQT induction before September 1999 when statutory induction was introduced.

7　Experienced teachers gave up some of their allocation of non-contact time in order to provide classroom cover for an NQT's 10 per cent release time. In contrast to state schools, supply teachers were rarely used.

8　Slightly fewer induction tutors have been delegated the lead role for assessment by their Principal in independent schools than in state schools.

---

*Box 4.2* Summary of our research findings for independent schools

Overall, induction for NQTs in independent schools appears to have improved since it became statutory in 1999 even more significantly than in other sectors. This is because there were fewer systems already in place. Three-quarters of independent school induction tutors thought that statutory induction had helped professional continuity and progression to a substantial or quite substantial extent. Just 2 per cent thought that it had not helped at all. Ninety-five per cent of independent schools said that introducing statutory induction had formalised, given clear structure or added rigour to their practices and school policies.

### Improving induction in independent schools

Case study 1 and Case study 2 are good examples of the effects of induction on an independent school and on an individual NQT. The cases are markedly different, however, in how induction is organised.

**Case study 1: an independent primary school**
Induction in the school was thoroughly revised in order to comply with statutory arrangements. It used to consist of one meeting between the deputy head and NQT after the first half term. It has 'come on in leaps and bounds', said the Principal.

The current NQT had carried out observations in three classes, one each term, and had been observed by three different colleagues.

Release time for this NQT is usually at the same time each week and was organised the previous summer through 'enhanced staffing', such as asking a part-time teacher to work an extra half day a week. When activities are on other days, experienced colleagues cover the NQT's class, using their existing allocation of non-contact time. Despite occasionally losing their non-contact time, the Principal and experienced teachers are enthusiastic about induction because of the positive learning experiences it has brought to all. This is why so many different staff are encouraged to be involved.

The management of induction in this school is very good. For example, colleagues who observed or hosted observations were selected because their area of expertise linked best to the NQT's own targets. These practical measures instituted by the Principal work to the advantage of all staff and foster an ethos of ongoing learning for all. Furthermore, the characteristics of low input by an Appropriate Body and high level of non-contact time for teachers which are typical in many independent schools, are used to their full advantage.

**Case study 2: a secondary NQT**

This NQT saw induction as a repeat of her PGCE. She told us, 'I shouldn't have to prove myself again' by passing more standards. Her school did little to clarify and address this concern. Unfortunately, targets written at the end of her PGCE course were still being used a term into her induction period. Also, she grew anxious about being observed by her induction tutor because she thought that the tutor emphasised summative assessment at the expense of constructive support and monitoring.

This situation would have improved if time had been spent on building closer, more open working relationships early on, and the induction tutor was given at least one period a week of non-contact time that coincided with the NQT's release time. Giving a further member of staff a formal supporting role could have helped as an outlet for concerns, too.

## Special schools

There are very few NQTs working in special schools. However, if they do work in the special sector in their first year they must undergo induction and the school must provide it. The induction period for NQTs working in all maintained and non-maintained special schools is exactly the same as for other state schools. There are no extra rules or conditions. However, our research found that the particular characteristics of special schools slightly alter induction practices and procedures.

In special schools, induction needs managing sensitively so that induction tutors and NQTs feel that they can take necessary time out of the classroom and that children are not unsettled by unfamiliar teachers providing the cover. One head teacher managed this situation by building up a good relationship with a supply teacher agency which she feels knows her requirements very well.

Our research suggested that special school teachers are perhaps more comfortable with face-to-face training and guidance than other schools. They felt they had very little time to read and think through for themselves the key induction documents – the DfEE circular, TTA Supporting Induction booklets and Appropriate Body publications. There was a strong call for more accessible support courses. They thought that this would be a good use of INSET days because their full attention could be given over to induction. Others found emailing questions to Appropriate Bodies was useful because they did not have to leave the school premises.

- The amount of contact different special schools had with their Appropriate Bodies varied. Some had weekly contact; some once per year but 22 per cent did not use Appropriate Bodies or any other external source for training and guidance at all.
- When Appropriate Bodies were used, they were particularly useful in reviewing objectives, observing NQTs, giving feedback and helping conduct formal assessments.
- Special school induction tutors and head teachers felt rather isolated from others doing similar roles, because there was little opportunity to leave their own class during lesson time or after school.
- Induction tutors in special schools had significantly less previous experience of working with NQTs than those in state schools.
- Half the induction tutors were allocated release time for their induction role, whereas in non-special schools it was less than one-third.
- Most special schools covered the NQTs' release time internally, as using supply teachers who were unfamiliar with the pupils was naturally even more problematic than in other settings.

*Box 4.3* Summary of our research findings for special schools

## Small schools

Statutory induction for small schools is exactly the same as for other state schools. There is one extra piece of guidance of particular relevance to small schools in the DfEE induction circular. When the head teacher is also the induction tutor and has 'undertaken all the observation of the NQT ... consideration should be given to ways in which a third party may be involved in providing evidence so that the assessment can be shown to be fair' (DfEE 2000a: para. 64).

Although there were only a few small schools (under 100 pupils) in our research we found a number of areas where induction was different from other schools. The specific concerns raised about NQTs in small schools need addressing through careful management of induction.

### Improving induction in small schools

Perhaps the main challenge that needs addressing when induction is provided in small schools is the breaking down of isolation typically experienced by both NQTs and induction tutors. This is illustrated in the case study on page 49.

The way that small schools successfully address their problems is to include as many people as possible in supporting their NQT's induction. Here are some ideas that we came across. Schools could:

- Where the induction tutor was also the head teacher, the Appropriate Body had visited the school to observe the NQT. This, however, was no different to many schools which are now visited to assist support, monitoring and assessment.
- Head teachers had a regular class teaching responsibility ranging from 50 per cent to a 100 per cent of a timetable. They felt particularly pressurised. Some felt unconfident that they had fully carried out their induction role.
- NQTs were appointed to very small schools primarily because they were the cheapest staffing option but also to bring in 'fresh, young blood' with up-to-date knowledge of curricular and educational matters.
- Meeting all the induction standards and receiving support from colleagues is a difficulty for the NQTs in small schools. This is because of the isolation experienced. Planning was identified as a particular difficulty for the NQTs with multiple age groups in a class and no teachers of the same age groups to bounce ideas off.
- NQTs in small schools tended to teach higher than expected numbers of children with special educational needs because parents of such children had been attracted by small classes and the small school ethos.
- Finding time and resources for releasing staff to do observations is particularly problematic. Paying for supply cover took a relatively large proportion of a small school budget and established teachers had no non-contact time.

Box 4.4 Summary of findings for small schools

- appoint a governor for NQTs. For example, one school asked an experienced governor to help solve some specific problems identified by the NQT.
- make sure the NQT knows about and attends any meetings run by the Appropriate Body. This is especially important in the first term when social and emotional support from NQTs in other schools is most needed. This means planning for release time to coincide with Appropriate Body programmes.
- establish or join a local 'cluster' of schools that can provide a forum for sharing resources, networking and moderating induction. This can be for both induction tutors and NQTs, either separately or together.
- arrange for a suitably experienced teacher in another of the cluster schools to act as a 'buddy' to the NQT and/or induction tutor.
- find ways to create an ethos within the school which values time to talk to colleagues about professional matters. This can be seen as part of what is now known as 'promoting a learning culture' in schools.
- use the existing package of support, monitoring and assessment

**Case study: Gillian and Trevor**

Gillian is an NQT teaching fourteen Nursery, Reception and Year 1 children together in one classroom, which is a mobile hut in the playground. Trevor, her induction tutor, is also the head teacher and teaches a class on three days a week. They work in a remote village school of fifty-four children. Gillian is the only person teaching the Foundation Stage whilst the rest of the staff teach the national curriculum. She has never taught mixed ages before and takes a long time to differentiate sufficiently for the full span of ability.

Schemes of work were only in draft form when she arrived and in all types of planning she feels isolated. There is no one to bounce ideas off. She knows how busy her colleagues are with their multiple responsibilities and feels reluctant to ask for extra help. The situation is made worse in Gillian's mind by Trevor having been very careful to observe the induction regulation that NQTs should not have an unreasonable workload: additional responsibilities have been passed on to colleagues because she is an NQT.

Trevor also feels guilty that he snatches time where he can to support Gillian and so the provision she receives is *ad hoc* and largely informal. He tends to assess Gillian through reading her weekly plans and occasionally wandering into her classroom. Although he has a lot of teaching experience, he has never found the time to attend an induction tutor training course.

Gillian had a heavy burden upon her, not helped by the apparent lack of a structured induction programme. Like many NQTs, even though she was seen as a confident personality, she felt shy about asking for more constructive support. They would both have benefited from Trevor setting an atmosphere of open dialogue right at the beginning so that concerns could be aired. He also needed to take the whole induction process more seriously. One positive aspect of this situation was that Gillian felt that because her induction tutor was the head teacher she did not have to negotiate with more than one person when wanting to attend a course, for example.

offered by the Appropriate Body to the full. The LEA's induction support package was described as a 'life line' by an induction tutor in one small school. Here the Appropriate Body staff worked mainly via telephone and email because this was more convenient than travelling a long distance to the course centre. Support was given as and when needed. The school was also a member of a 'small school federation', which offered mutual support.

- work to establish open staff relations, so that all will seek support when they need it.

## Supply teachers

There are specific regulations that refer to NQTs who work as supply teachers, about which there is general confusion. An NQT on supply can and must undergo induction if they are in a placement on a regular timetable for a term or more in the same school. The term does not have to begin at any particular time. For example, it could begin a few weeks into one school term and carry on until a few weeks into the following term. Anything short of one term in length does not count towards induction. Nor can the start of an induction period be backdated once it is clear that an NQT will be staying for longer than a term. LEAs give schools £1,000 per term for any NQT on a term's supply to cover induction expenses, as they do for other NQTs.

However, induction cannot be served through short-term supply work – and there is a limit on how long NQTs can do this work before they start induction. No more than a year and a term can be worked on engagements of less than one term. This period begins when an NQT takes up the first placement as a short-term supply teacher, and is measured in calendar terms from that point, rather than an aggregation of work. NQTs do not have to have done much supply work. From the first day they work the clock starts ticking. This time limit is known as the 'four-term rule'. When the induction period is undertaken in more than one school or college, Appropriate Bodies and head teachers have to make sure that all records get passed on.

Supply agencies do not have any legal responsibilities regarding induction. However, a new Quality Mark for supply agencies has been introduced and a range of supportive good practice was found to exist. One company supports NQTs through:

- advice and personal support,
- personal development action planning,
- an induction placement opportunity,
- pay in line with common pay scale,
- long-term and permanent placements,
- opportunity to network with other NQTs,
- three NQT seminars, free of charge:
  - Teachers & the Law
  - Classroom Management
  - Professional Development.

NQTs are assigned a personal consultant who will help find a placement for the induction period and will maintain regular contact with the NQT, monitor progress and develop a proactive role. The consultant will discuss the Career Entry Profile with the NQT and helps them set targets for development.

Confusions about doing induction on supply are numerous. Five common errors are that:

1   NQTs can do supply without doing induction for as long as they like.
2   They cannot do induction as a supply teacher.
3   Supply teachers on induction do not get a 10 per cent reduction in timetable.
4   Once they have done one term towards their induction the four-term time limit starts again. They have another four terms of short-term supply before having to do another full term in one school.
5   No one will know if an NQT breaks the four-term rule.

Our research found numerous confusions about the 'four-term rule'. Some of these appear below, with the correct information where appropriate.

---

- There is a widespread, general confusion around statutory induction and supply teaching.
- The four-term rule has proved especially difficult to interpret accurately. It is very widely and consistently misunderstood.
- The number of NQTs on supply has decreased sharply since the introduction of statutory induction. Induction actively discourages NQTs from going on supply.
- Some head teachers do not know that NQTs working on supply for at least a term in a school should be on induction and that the school can claim £1,000 per term to fund their reduced timetable and other induction costs.
- When supply teacher agencies use the term 'induction' they often mean an introduction to the English education system for teachers from abroad rather than statutory induction for NQTs.
- Several supply agencies did not know about the four-term rule.
- Some supply agencies actively seek induction placements on an NQT's behalf, but others do not. After initial placement in a school, supply agencies tend to play a minimal role but some have resource centres and counselling services.

---

Box 4.5 Evidence from our research on induction and supply teachers

1   'I thought that NQTs had five years to complete induction. I knew nothing about four terms.' This is a general lack of awareness about induction for supply teachers ('The *what* rule?').

    There is no time limit between gaining QTS and starting induction but NQTs can only do short-term supply for four terms.

2   'In effect the four-term rule means an NQT can do one year on supply and then have one term to find a one-year post so that he or she can do induction.'

    This is certainly possible, but there are many ways of putting together patterns of work. For example, one term of induction during the first four terms of teaching then another two terms after the four terms has ended.

3   'NQTs must start induction after four terms after finishing their initial teacher education course.'

    The four terms start from the first day of supply teaching, not when QTS was gained. Thus, teachers can go travelling or teach abroad after gaining QTS, then come back as supply teachers and do induction.

4   'NQTs can do a maximum of four terms on day-to-day supply, no more. They need to start induction after this time and have two further years in which to complete it.' This is almost correct, except that there is no two-year time limit.

5   'NQTs need to complete their induction *within* four terms.' Not correct: the four-term rule only applies to supply teaching.

6   'I'm on supply in a school for a term but don't want to do induction there.' If NQTs are working in a school for a term they *must* be undergoing induction.

### Improving induction for supply teaching NQTs

Spending the first year of teaching as a supply teacher is not easy. In fact, induction has already deterred a great number of NQTs from going into supply teaching. However, there are still a number of NQTs for whom supply teaching is the most suitable option. Some want to 'test out' whether teaching is really for them and to get to know a range of schools so that they can make an informed choice when vacancies arise. Some NQTs wish to pursue careers in relatively insecure professions such as acting or art and do supply work to supplement their income. Others would like a long-term position but cannot find one because there are few vacancies in their locality and their family commitments restrict how far they can travel.

## What people need to know about the four-term rule

The following six points aim to clarify the complexities of the four-term rule.

1    There is *no* time limit for when a teacher has to *start* induction.
2    There *is* a time limit, which starts on the very first day that supply teaching is done.
3    This time limit is four terms. So, from the first day of supply teaching – whether this is a 'one-off' day in a school, a few days and then a long gap with no teaching, or a longer-term placement – the clock starts ticking.
4    NQTs have four terms in which they can do placements of less than one term in length. Anything less than one term cannot count towards induction.
5    After four terms, the only teaching that can be done at all in a state school is that which counts towards induction. No more teaching can be done, even one day of supply teaching, unless it is on an agreed induction placement of a full term.
6    Once an NQT has passed induction she or he can do as much supply teaching of any length as they like.

## Possible timetables for doing induction on supply

Although the number of NQTs working as supply teachers has fallen, there are some who have no choice and who are unsure of what will happen if they have not completed three terms of induction by the time their four terms of supply work has been used up, as in this account:

> I completed my PGCE in June 2000 and spent July and the early part of the autumn term on supply. I then took a maternity post and completed one term of my induction in Spring 2001. After that I went back to short-term supply. Towards the end of Autumn 2001 I will take up another maternity post, which the school have said will count towards my induction. When that comes to an end what will be my position? If I can't get a long-term or permanent post, should I be looking for a job outside teaching? This would be a great shame, as I love doing the job, but nevertheless have a mortgage and children to support. There are no shortages of my subject in my area, and because I have a family, I can't move.

Table 4.1 gives examples of termly timetables for three NQTs who gained their QTS at the same time and were doing induction (at least partially) on supply.

Table 4.1 Examples of how three NQTs working as supply teachers completed induction

| NQT | Term 1 | Term 2 | Term 3 | Term 4 | Term 5 | Term 6 | Term 7 | Term 8 |
|---|---|---|---|---|---|---|---|---|
| NQT 1 | 1st induction term | 1 day of supply (four-term limit begins) | 2nd induction term | 3rd induction term | | | | |
| NQT 2 | Supply for second half of the term | No teaching | No teaching | No teaching | Wants to do supply but four terms used up | 1st induction term | 2nd induction term | 3rd induction term |
| NQT 3 | No teaching | 1st induction term | 2nd induction term on supply | 3rd induction term incomplete as leaves before end | Short-term supply | Short-term supply | Four-term limit is reached. Cannot teach | 3rd induction term finished |

NQTs on supply are potentially vulnerable. Some will not have jobs organised by the end of their training because they are worried about whether they would pass the course. Their under-developed teaching skills and the resulting lack of confidence mean that that they are unlikely to succeed in the demanding environment of short-term supply work. They usually start induction during the school year, instead of in September when the majority of NQTs start. This can cause additional problems, for example:

- their induction tutors have not attended the key training at the beginning of the year,
- they miss the most pertinent LEA induction sessions, such as those on classroom management and planning,
- they do not receive their induction entitlement, either because the school does not want to invest time and effort into someone who is only going to be there for a term,
- cover for the 10 per cent reduced timetable is hard to provide particularly for classes which have already been disrupted,
- they take time to get used to the school's systems.

Schools with an induction policy and experience of the regulations will be well placed to manage the induction of a supply teacher. Martin, in the case study below, was lucky in going to a school which supported him well.

**Case study: Martin**

Martin did not manage to get a teaching post before finishing his BA(Ed) and so registered with a supply agency in order to find work. On Martin's request, the agency found a school that agreed to provide induction. He started teaching four weeks into the autumn term. Fortunately, there were other NQTs already in the school so Martin could fit in with their induction programme, otherwise arrangements would have been hasty and ill-prepared.

Some concerns were raised early on as to Martin's teaching ability. The induction tutor increased the support and monitoring for Martin. His head teacher thought that not all schools would necessarily want to see Martin through his induction because he was on a supply contract and had taken up additional staff time. But he did complete induction successfully and the induction tutor felt he made a good contribution to the teaching profession.

# Chapter 5

# The induction tutor role

For statutory induction to work, the role of the induction tutor is crucial. They are members of staff chosen by the head teacher 'to provide day to day monitoring and support' for the NQT (DfEE 2000a: para. 1) and are key to the provision of statutory induction. The circular states that they should be:

> fully aware of the requirements of the induction period and should have the necessary skills, expertise and knowledge to work effectively in the role. In particular, the induction tutor should be able to make rigorous and fair judgements about the NQT's performance in relation to the requirement for satisfactory completion of the induction period and to provide or coordinate guidance and effective support for the NQT's professional development.
>
> (DfEE 2000a: para. 26)

This chapter will deal with the role of the induction tutor and the skills and professional knowledge they need; day-to-day management of induction within the school; what constitutes a good induction programme; and issues of resourcing, time and organisation of the programme. The induction tutor's role and duties in the setting and reviewing of objectives, in lesson observation and in formal assessment, are dealt with in other chapters of this book.

## Skills of an induction tutor

To fulfil their statutory obligations and to contribute to the NQT's development and support, induction tutors need to have a wide range of skills, knowledge and experience, including in-depth understanding of the standards for QTS and the induction standards, and of the contexts of education and professional development. They also need an ability to relate their understanding and experience to the individual NQT's context. The dual nature of the role, both support and assessor, adds to its demands for practical knowledge and understanding. Thus there are tensions in the role of support, monitoring and assessment, as one induction tutor said:

> You have to set up a relationship with NQTs in which they feel that they can tell you what difficulties they're experiencing, but you must back that up with your own observation and you have to develop a relationship in which you are able to give praise but also constructive criticism. But you also have to be prepared, and go into the relationship with each NQT knowing that it's possible that this NQT will fail ... So it's a delicate relationship.

The TTA, working with a group of practitioners, have defined effective induction tutors as:

- confident in their understanding of the characteristics of high-quality learning and teaching in the classroom,
- aware of how different learners learn and able to recognise the different learning styles of particular NQTs,
- confident about their own teaching,
- open minded and receptive to new ideas and approaches,
- experienced in evaluating evidence, including through classroom observation,
- good communicators who are genuinely committed to supporting the development of others,
- prepared to acknowledge their own development needs and take steps to address them,
- able to use a range of helping strategies, including providing constructive feedback and engaging in positive dialogue with the NQT.

(TTA 2001b: 6)

Although this seems like a great deal to expect, most of the induction tutors we met in our research had all these characteristics. In their day-to-day work with NQTs, we found that induction tutors also managed to:

- respect new teachers as professionals,
- take time to explain and map out the stages of the induction year,
- encourage and enable NQTs to take increasing responsibility for their own development,
- recognise and celebrate achievements,
- be open and honest about areas for improvement,
- support NQTs in making the identified improvements,
- be aware of the strategies that can be used to provide additional support if an NQT is experiencing difficulties,
- support the process by efficient time management and record keeping.

(TTA 2001b: 7)

## How the induction tutor role is organised

In Chapter 3 we discussed how schools managed the induction tutor role. In some schools one tutor takes the role but in many others aspects are shared. We found that this occurred in 82 per cent of state schools and 50 per cent of independent schools. Slightly more secondary than primary induction tutors shared provision (secondary 94 per cent; primary 84 per cent).

In schools with more than one NQT it is common practice to appoint an induction coordinator, although there is no mention of such a role in the DfES regulations or original TTA guidance. We found that the induction management role had a range of titles, such as:

- Staff Development Officer,
- Professional Tutor,
- Teacher Coordinator,
- Induction Coordinator,
- INSET Manager/Coordinator.

The latest guidance for induction tutors from the TTA acknowledges this role and entitles it 'Induction Manager' (TTA 2001b). This is helpful in reflecting the practice of almost all secondary and some primary schools. It was clear from our research that the lack of a clearly defined coordinating role in the policy has caused some confusion in schools, particularly concerning responsibility for the assessment reports. In some schools these are written by the head of department and in others they are the responsibility of this overall coordinator.

One secondary school induction coordinator we visited had exemplary practice. His schoolwide responsibilities were to:

- update the induction policy and have an overview of the whole process of induction,
- explain new procedures, and disseminate useful documentation,
- appoint induction tutors (usually the NQT's head of department) and arrange for their training,
- be a point of contact for all staff on induction issues,
- keep the head teacher informed, and arrange for her to observe each NQT once during the year,
- liaise with the LEA.

He worked to ensure the smooth running of the programme, by:

- ensuring that meetings between the induction tutors and the NQT took place once a week throughout the year, suggesting topics such as those in Table 5.1,

**20 September**
The induction tutor's role in support, monitoring and the assessment of the induction standards
Understanding the Career Entry Profile
Setting the first objectives
How to make the first observation
Setting up a school-based induction programme
The accreditation of this course

**18 October**
Procedures for recording work as induction tutor
The school-based induction programme
Observation and feedback skills
Setting and reviewing objectives for the QTS standards

**8 November**
Planning, teaching and class management standards 1
Observation and feedback skills
Setting and reviewing objectives
Adults as learners

**29 November**
Assessing the NQT against the standards
Writing the end of term report on the NQT
Conducting the end of term assessment meeting
Setting and reviewing objectives

**17 January**
Feedback on the completed assessment forms
Planning, teaching and class management standards 2
Observation and feedback skills
Setting and reviewing objectives
Reviewing the school-based programme

**28 February**
Monitoring, assessment, recording, reporting and accountability standards
Assessment and feedback skills
Setting and reviewing objectives
Tricky situations

**28 March**
Other professional requirements standards:
Observation and feedback skills
Setting and reviewing objectives
Writing the end of term report on the NQT

**23 May**
Preparing for the final assessment meeting
Procedures for weak NQTs
Writing the final report to feed in to performance management
Review of your school policy

*Box 5.1* An LEA Induction Tutor Training Programme

*Table 5.1* Example of areas for heads of department to discuss with NQTs. The third column records the proposed learning outcomes for the new teachers

| | | |
|---|---|---|
| Faculty issues and meetings | • pre-discussion<br>• contribution<br>• understanding policy | The team's philosophy, policies and practice. |
| Curriculum planning and assessment | • how children learn<br>• setting strategies<br>• scheme of work<br>• resources<br>• assessing concepts<br>• assessing skills<br>• NC | Putting the team's beliefs about learning in our subject area into practice. This includes making the most of pupils, materials and records. |
| Classroom management | • safety<br>• equipment<br>• displays<br>• desks<br>• classroom strategies<br>• seating plans<br>• tone<br>• rules/codes<br>• detention<br>• diaries<br>• referrals<br>• communicating with home<br>• use of register<br>• corridor<br>• prioritising | Making sure that all your positive ideas don't founder because the pupils can't find the equipment they need!<br><br>Creating and maintaining a positive working environment.<br><br>Ensuring that curriculum planning is put into practice for all children in the class.<br><br>Developing strategies so that you maintain control of learning.<br><br>Taking appropriate follow-up action outside lesson time. |
| Monitoring | • work rate<br>• homework<br>• attendance and punctuality<br>• behaviour | Input and outcomes.<br><br>Ensuring that equal opportunities for learning are put into practice. |
| School and faculty organisation | • physical<br>• responsibility structure<br>• procedures<br>• role of unions | Knowing the system/structures in use in the school and when and how to use them. |
| Using the team | • seeking help/advice<br>• role as learner<br>• role as new teacher<br>• team's responsibility | Making best use of all members of the team, both formally and informally. |
| Outside the team | • tone/style<br>• appropriate dealings<br>• representation of team<br>• working with support services<br>• tutoring | Making best use of other adults, both formally and informally.<br><br>Knowing when and how to deal with people outside the team. |

*Table 5.1* Continued

| Faculty issues and meetings | • pre-discussion<br>• contribution<br>• understanding policy | The team's philosophy, policies and practice. |
| --- | --- | --- |
| The school year and deadlines | • anticipating/meeting deadlines<br>• record-keeping<br>• bulletin<br>• diary/notebook | Knowing what's coming up and what to do to be ready for it. |
| Making time ... | • marking<br>• upkeep of room<br>• pupils<br>• team<br>• yourself<br>• arriving and leaving<br>• fatigue and stress<br>• sleep | How to prioritise and fit all the work in whilst still having a life. |

- helping where heads of department were unable to support their NQT, because of sickness for instance,
- giving general support to all the NQTs, making sure he spoke to them informally every day in the staffroom,
- arranging for the NQTs to visit other teachers and schools,
- running a programme of professional development for the group of NQTs, including arranging different speakers.

His assessment and quality control role meant that he:

- monitored all the NQTs' progress,
- ensured consistency of entitlement across departments,
- completed the assessment forms – or ensured that the heads of department completed them to a consistent standard.

All those induction managers who were responsible for four or more NQTs shared the provision of induction with a number of other staff, such as subject leaders, heads of department, SENCOs or parallel teachers. The need for help with the NQT's subject or age phase was particularly emphasised. The following quotation from an induction manager illustrates how and why the roles were divided:

> The induction tutor is regarded as a combination of myself [deputy head] and the heads of department and the split of responsibilities is really along subject lines ... My role is to provide induction sessions

on things like the role of the tutor, school policies on assessment, equal opportunities, priorities for the school in terms of the school development plan and so on.

Problems arise, however, when the responsibilities of all involved are not clear or not carried out. In our research we came across NQTs who had fallen through the net, with each person in the induction tutor role assuming that someone else was taking the lead. This had severe practical consequences, such as an NQT who missed out on a much sought after induction course because the induction tutor and manager each assumed that the other had booked it.

NQTs appreciate having a variety of staff to learn from. One secondary NQT talked about the support from heads of year over behaviour issues. A primary NQT said 'the whole staff' helped her, particularly a 'fantastic' parallel class teacher and the Key Stage Coordinator. NQTs benefit from feeling valued and being supported by everyone on the staff, as this new teacher explains:

> They attempt to make sure that even as an NQT you're included and you can say: 'Look I think this' and it's quite easy to do that, which is very, very important. I think to feel that you're actually part of the staff is a big issue so I'm really happy that we are involved in discussion, the whole staff, we talk about things. ... Even my classroom assistants are fantastic. So everyone helps.

Another NQT testified how useful it is to have a 'buddy mentor', whether informally or formally:

> to speak to somebody who's not in your department, or ... other people who are, who haven't been here for years and who are seeing the problems that they've had and how they've overcome them.

Several NQTs explained how the staff as a whole, together with good LEA support, can make for a positive induction experience:

> I was very well supported by the head of school, who understood exactly what I was expected to achieve, and also other members of staff. The local LEA provided constructive and comprehensive courses which supported my learning ... The people around me were so good.

## Experience to do the role

From our research we know that induction tutors are predominantly senior teachers in their schools, although this finding disguises a wide range of people in the role. A small number are head teachers, generally in small primary schools. However, nearly a third describe themselves as 'just' classroom teachers.

Induction tutors come with a range of experience. They are often responsible for trainee teachers. Two-thirds of secondary and half of primary induction tutors had expertise in supporting trainees on teaching practice. It is interesting that in both phases induction tutors were more used to working with trainee teachers than with NQTs. Over half of the induction tutors in the secondary sector and two-thirds in the primary sector had not had responsibility for NQTs before statutory induction was introduced.

Experience with trainees or arrangements before induction was made statutory is clearly very useful but it can cause problems. There are great similarities between old and new induction practices, and initial training and induction. However, the differences are significant too. Induction tutors need to keep up to date and be fully conversant with the requirements of statutory induction. OFSTED found that 'many schools were building on previous good practice in supporting NQTs or ITT trainees', adding that 'this sometimes meant that they did not see the need to provide training that was specifically focused on the induction standards' (OFSTED 2001c: para. 37). We found instances where the induction tutor appeared very experienced but was unclear about the procedures involved in objective setting, in assessment against the induction standards and, indeed, with the basic statutory requirements. The school induction policy had not been updated since statutory induction was introduced.

In several schools, induction tutors frequently referred to the NQTs as 'students' and put them with the initial teacher education students for training sessions. Naturally, the NQTs resented what appeared to be an undermining of their status, and clearly their needs are different.

## Sources of support and training

Induction tutors need support and training in the role. As well as the immediate benefits for the NQTs, support and training in this role will develop their capacity for wider involvement in the school's leadership and management. In particular, they will:

- develop experience and skills that are directly transferable to other management roles and responsibilities,
- have opportunities to reflect on approaches to achieving quality in teaching and learning, and how to improve their own teaching and that of colleagues.

(TTA 2001: 10)

Unfortunately we found that 16 per cent of induction tutors had not attended any type of course related to their role. This is a concern if we consider the required levels of knowledge, skills and understanding. Induction tutors should be entitled to high-quality professional development and the opportunity to undertake this. Box 5.1 shows one LEA's induction tutor training course that was spread throughout the year and which formed the basis of a strong network. It was held in the afternoons following some of the NQT sessions, in order to make best use of supply teacher cover in school. As the course was accredited by a university, participants could gain 20 credits towards an Advanced Diploma or MA in Education. This is an excellent way of raising the status of the induction tutor role and rewarding those people who undertake it.

## Ineffective induction tutors

Many NQTs in our research spoke highly of their induction tutors and other staff who had supported them. However, new teachers suffer when induction tutors are not effective or where the staff as a whole are not supportive. One respondent told us how the school as a whole was ill-prepared for implementing statutory induction but that the broad base of otherwise effective colleagues made a difference:

> I do not feel that my development was really a reflection on the induction tutor but more because of the support of my colleagues. There were no meetings arranged for NQTs or introductions to other new staff, etc.

This NQT said she was 'thrown in at the deep end and expected to have read the handbook!' Her colleagues' attitudes of awareness, genuine concern and empathy were appreciated. Her key recommendation was to make sure that 'all staff have reassurance as their main message' when communicating to NQTs: 'It was staff with this attitude that helped me successfully through the first year.'

One secondary NQT epitomised someone who had a bad experience on many fronts in her first year. Responsibility for her induction was shared between one of the deputy heads and the head of department. The former was too busy to do anything but complete end of term assessment forms. The latter was unhappy in the school and left at the end of the autumn term having given the NQT little support. As the post remained vacant for the rest of the school year, the NQT not only had to struggle on as the only full-time member of the department, but also had to organise lessons for supply teachers. At the end of the year she was contemplating not only leaving the school but the profession. The lack of anyone fulfilling the induction role meant that the NQT's job made unreasonable demands on her (see Table 5.2), and that no one helped or remedied the situation.

Table 5.2 One NQT's job compared to what the induction circular lays down

| NQTs should have a job that . . . | The NQT's experience |
| --- | --- |
| a Does not demand teaching outside the age range and subject(s) for which the NQT has been trained. | Compliance |
| b Does not present the NQT on a day-to-day basis with acute or especially demanding discipline problems. | Discipline was a significant problem in the school. The NQT had great problems controlling the pupils and very little help. |
| c Involves regular teaching of the same class(es). | Yes, but the NQT taught 16 different classes a week and did not get the reduced timetable until half way through the year. |
| d Involves similar planning, teaching and assessment processes to those in which teachers working in substantive posts in the school are engaged. | Had no head of department for the spring and summer terms and little help from her in the autumn term. The only other teacher in the department was part-time, so the NQT had to support supply teachers. |
| e Does not involve additional non-teaching responsibilities without the provision of appropriate preparation and support. | The NQT was a form tutor, but had no support. |

An ineffective head of department is described by one induction coordinator as 'the weak link':

> And that's the inconsistency, some heads of department are very good and take their responsibilities very seriously and do really work hard for the NQTs, and they really do see themselves as helping them to settle. And there are those that say: 'Well you know, when I came in I was just thrown in at the deep end, and that's the best way. That's what happened to me and you see, look I'm fine.'

Induction managers need to audit the school's provision, to see that provision is consistent for all the NQTs and that they all receive their entitlement. OFSTED found that, in half of the secondary schools where there was more than one NQT, the quality of support received by individual NQTs varied considerably between subject departments, particularly in the opportunities for NQTs to observe and work with experienced teachers. These variations in the quality of training often related to the quality of individual departments (OFSTED 2001c: para. 34).

One induction tutor testified to the effectiveness of the induction manager:

> X is very, very competent. He knows exactly what he's doing with the mentoring this year. Last year I didn't get very clear signals from the person who occupied this post before, so it's been a lot easier for me this year to get on top of it.

We have evidence of good induction tutors attempting to address this issue:

> If there is a case where I think that the head of department may not be effective in support I will normally ask a second person to act as a critical friend whilst the head of department remains with the responsibility for the internal assessment.

It is important for the induction tutor to be proactive in talking to other staff involved in induction provision. For instance it was only through discussion that an induction manager discovered that an NQT had taught the same lesson for both her and the head of department's observation.

## Workload

> It would seem to be an oversight that while the NQT was entitled to a reduced timetable there was no commensurate provision for the induction tutor to carry out their role.
>
> (Lewis and Varley 2000: 10)

OFSTED found that almost all school staff supporting NQTs did so in their existing non-contact time or after school. Bubb also found that induction tutors thought they needed much more dedicated time to do the job (Bubb 2000b: 4). Our research discovered that:

- 69 per cent of induction tutors had no specific release time for carrying out their role,
- 31 per cent had release time,
- the most common amount of release time allocated was between half an hour to an hour per week,
- the number of hours spent on the induction of NQTs was greater than classroom release time received,
- all induction tutors in secondary schools received extra salary points for the role, compared to only 8 per cent in primary schools.

There is a consensus (Earley and Kinder 1994; Maynard 1995; Simco 2000; Heilbronn and Jones 1997) that the role of the mentor/induction tutor is central but very demanding, requiring a great deal of both time and training, and that it needs to be given sufficient status and importance in schools. The NUT recommends that induction tutors should be allowed at least a half day release from teaching duties every alternate week to fulfil their role (NUT 2000b: 2). As a result of our research we recommended to the DfES that there should be dedicated, regular, funded time for induction tutors to carry out their role. We found only one LEA which gave any earmarked funding for the induction tutor role – £250 for a year. Although this gesture was appreciated, it only paid for about one and a third days out of the classroom.

The majority of induction tutors in our research were responsible for one NQT. However, in the state sector approximately one-fifth of the sample had five NQTs or more. This clearly has a great impact on the amount of work involved. One secondary head teacher spoke of workload difficulties with three NQTs in one department:

> They each have a separate mentor, which has not been easy, to be honest. Because obviously you need to first of all pick suitable people who've got suitable experience and are suitably good at that role and secondly you are actually asking them to do something completely unpaid, so we've tended to ask people who are already on some kind of incremental point; but even that, it is quite a demand.

He cited the case of a colleague who had agreed to be an induction tutor based on her experience prior to statutory induction. However, when she realised how much work was involved, she was unhappy about the role. So, the head teacher arranged for the role to be shared with the head of faculty.

If an NQT needs extra support, the workload implications are even greater. One primary induction tutor had an NQT who had failed his first assessment in another school. The induction tutor then worked closely with the NQT, setting monthly objectives:

> My role is very much one of supporting but also it's especially important in this situation that I've had to set very close targets to ensure that the NQT does achieve the standards required of him … It's added to the strain of everything else I have to do in my role.

There is much evidence to show that many staff involved in induction are dedicated and devote their own time in order to develop and retain staff, often without being given time or financial reward. Some induction tutors and head teachers suggested accrediting the work involved, which would go some way to acknowledging the amount of time, effort and goodwill involved in doing the job well. Another way of managing the workload is for induction tutors to see this alongside other roles in the school. It will be evident that the knowledge and skills needed to undertake this role will transfer to other aspects of the work of experienced teachers and those with other management roles: for example, curriculum or phase coordinators, subject leaders, heads of department and senior management.

## Induction tutors' views of their job

Despite the time constraints on their work and other resourcing implications, many induction tutors we spoke to enjoyed the role. Some said, 'It's one of the parts of my job that I enjoy the most.' It is certainly a vital role in the induction process. Most induction tutors find the role rewarding, though one induction tutor pointed out that she needed 'to make an enormous conceptual leap, because we forget what it's like to be a new teacher, and most of us, certainly at my age, didn't have any kind of induction or support'.

Many induction tutors valued working with NQTs, for the innovations which new teachers can bring:

> In the vast majority of cases, they're young people who are enthusiastic, enjoy their work, and you know I find it very refreshing and I learn from watching them. I think this is the thing that's perhaps surprising, an experienced teacher can go and watch an NQT and still pick up some tricks.

NQTs are often seen as a positive asset to the school. One induction tutor with previous experience of mentoring NQTs in another school consciously sought to appoint an NQT 'to bring fresh blood' into the school, and reflected that preparing work for NQTs supported whole school development. For instance, in one school a teacher put together a training document for NQTs that was then disseminated to the whole staff.

On the whole, induction tutors considered that the procedures for statutory induction were an improvement on past arrangements:

> Clearly the system now is much more formal which to some extent is good because it allows me to do continuous monitoring.

> On the whole it's a good programme. I think it's important to have this period of induction ... it's an important process which I think is well structured.

However, there were a number of people who disliked elements of statutory induction such as:

- the tension between supporting on the one hand and monitoring and assessing on the other,

- accountability made them anxious about paperwork – they did not know how much they should be recording,
- the role took a great deal of time but had low status,
- the consequences of failure were too severe.

## Setting up induction programmes

The induction regulations state:

> Planned professional development activities should be based on the strengths and areas for professional development identified in the Career Entry Profile, as well as on any new or revised objectives that are agreed at review discussions during the year. They should be focused on helping the NQT to meet the Induction Standards. When compiling a programme of support, induction tutors will wish to consider arrangements for the NQT to:
>
> a   receive information about the school, the specific post and the arrangements for induction, in advance of the first day in post;
> b   receive information about their rights and responsibilities and those of others involved and the nature and purpose of assessment in the induction period;
> c   participate in the school's general induction arrangements for new staff;
> d   take part in any programme of staff training at the school, for example on the national literacy or numeracy strategies;
> e   know about any whole school policies, including those on child protection, management of behaviour and health and safety, and contribute, with other teachers, to specific school improvement activities;
> f   spend time with the school's SENCO to focus on specific and general SEN matters;
> g   receive, where appropriate, training development or advice from professionals from outside the school, e.g. from other schools, LEAs, Higher Education Institutions, Diocesan authorities, professional bodies and subject associations;
> h   attend external training events that are relevant to identified individual needs.
>
> (DfEE 2000a: paras 51–2)

OFSTED found that three-quarters of the primary schools and half of the secondary schools provided good training for all NQTs. The OFSTED inspection found that key staff in schools 'had a very good understanding of the QTS and induction standards and had planned the induction programme to ensure that the NQTs achieved these' (OFSTED 2001c: para. 34). Our research had similar findings. There were common features to successful induction programmes.

## Features of an effective programme

### Pre-employment induction

An induction visit before starting work is valued by NQTs. Some schools organise an unpaid or paid induction day or week in July for all new teachers, including those who are newly qualified. One school who paid for new staff to be put up in a local hotel felt that the expense was justified in terms of the valuable bonding that took place. It also helped to prepare new staff adequately for the start of the new year. One NQT said: 'It was good to meet people properly, spend some time with the head of department, get schemes of work.' Another NQT said: 'We got all the information and had a couple of months to go away and mull it over and work out what it all meant.'

### Regular meetings with individual NQTs

The majority of induction tutors in our research held meetings lasting at least 30 minutes with an NQT at least fortnightly (27 per cent held them weekly, 26 per cent fortnightly and 37 per cent half termly). Only 2 per cent reported having no meetings.

The vast majority of NQTs in our research were able to meet with their induction tutors. Where it was not possible to timetable different members of staff to be free at the same time, induction tutors arranged meetings after school. One primary school organised non-contact time for all three NQTs and the induction tutor on the same afternoon. They met as a group, talked about issues and had individual tutorial sessions.

However, we found that NQTs thought that meetings were taking place less regularly than did the induction tutors. We believe there is a lesson to be learnt here about clear communication over the programme of activities, and sticking to an agreed schedule. Publishing the schedule in advance is highly recommended good practice.

Most NQTs had scheduled weekly or fortnightly meetings to discuss issues and progress. The most common topics of these meetings were:

- feedback after lesson observation,
- behaviour management,
- the curriculum,
- schemes of work and lesson planning,
- school development,
- parents' evenings.

### Group meetings for all the NQTs

Where there are several NQTs in a school, it is useful to hold group meetings on topics of interest to all. Figure 5.1 shows one school's general programme which coordinated with the LEA's induction programme. Another induction manager explains:

> One night a week for the first term we look at issues that are pertinent to school, then in the second and the third term we just do it a bit more ad hoc and look at various issues as they come up. For example this week it's their very first parents' evening. But they meet as a group because then they can also say, 'I had a terrible time this week' and I can help them or they can help each other, which is very important.

### Informal meetings

Informal meetings are also important. Over 80 per cent of induction tutors said they met informally and often daily with their NQTs, initiated by either party and covering a wide range of immediate concerns.

### Whole school INSET

Staff meetings and INSET days make a valuable contribution to NQTs' development. Box 5.3 shows how this can be recorded alongside other more individual activities.

### Induction provision from outside the school

Although the school was seen as a valuable source of specific support for NQTs, outside help brings expert and fresh perspectives. More than four out of every five (or 84 per cent) head teachers in state schools reported using sources from outside their own school to help provide induction for NQTs. The LEA was by far the most commonly used source. Most NQTs attended one or two courses, although some attended twelve throughout the year and others went on to residential courses. Most schools found the formal involvement of LEA induction staff in reviewing objectives, observing NQTs and conducting formal assessment helpful.

NQTs value the opportunity to meet with other NQTs outside their school. Peer group support plays a key role in validating NQTs' experiences, and helps them to succeed in the induction year:

> It's lovely when you speak to other reception teachers and they say exactly the same things and you think, that's super, because I know it's not just my children, it's not just me.

The meetings will take place on Tuesdays from 4.15 to 5.15. You are expected to attend all sessions, play an active role and will have the opportunity to raise issues of particular concern to you. Their aim is to help you successfully complete your Induction Year and to continue your professional development in relation to the targets set out in your Career Entry Profile and the particular context of the school. The school sessions will complement those organised by the LEA (printed in italics) and the regular sessions you will have with your department Induction Tutor.

| Date | Topic |
| --- | --- |
| Sep 5 | Welcome to the school |
| Sep 12 | NQT information session and get together |
| Sep 19 | Settling in – what you can expect |
| Sep 26 | *Pastoral care – working with parents – LEA* |
| Oct 10 | First half-term review |
| Oct 17 | *SEN and student support for learning and behaviour – LEA* |
| Nov 7 | A proactive approach to classroom management |
| Nov 14 | Gifted and talented initiative |
| Dec 5 | Raising the attainment of girls |
| Dec 12 | End of term review |
| Jan 16 | Assessment: serving learning |
| Jan 23 | *EAL/Partnership teaching – LEA* |
| Feb 13 | End of half-term review |
| Mar 6 | *Literacy and numeracy strategies – LEA* |
| Mar 27 | Accessing and using school data |
| Apr 2 | End of term review |
| May 1 | *ICT across the curriculum – strategies – LEA* |
| May 8 | To be decided by NQTs |
| May 22 | End of half-term review |
| Jun 12 | To be decided by NQTs |
| Jul 3 | Evaluation session and congratulations social |
| Jul 10 | End of year review: what's next? |

Box 5.2 An example of a secondary school group induction programme

| Objectives: | To write clear and informative reports for parents | | |
|---|---|---|---|
| | To conduct parents' evening confidently | | |
| | To plan an outing | | |

| Week beginning observation of NQT | NQT release time for induction | Induction tutor meetings | Staff meetings and INSET |
|---|---|---|---|
| **5 June** | Observe Y4 Written reflection | Plan the induction programme | Report writing formats, tips and agreed procedures |
| **12 June** Observation by induction tutor | Observe Y1 & Y2 in Beacon school, focusing on good practice Written reflection | Feedback from observation Reading reports | Moderation of science investigations for Years 1–6 |
| **19 June** | LEA induction course: professional development – being a curriculum coordinator | | School trips and outings – health and safety procedures incl. risk analysis |
| **26 June** Observation by head teacher | Preliminary visit to farm to prepare for class trip – risk assessment | Feedback from observation | Mathematics – the mental and oral starter |
| **3 July** | Prepare for class trip, using school policies | Discuss planning for the outing | Mathematics – purposeful plenary ideas |
| **10 July** Final assessment meeting | Gathering evidence for the final assessment meeting | Final assessment meeting | Sports Day arrangements |
| **17 July** | Looking at new class and their records | | Planning for next year |

*Box 5.3* A primary NQT's individual Induction Programme – 2nd half of summer term

## An individualised programme

The induction circular states:

> The induction period will combine an individualised programme of moni-
> toring and support, which provides opportunities for NQTs to develop
> further their knowledge, skills and achievements in relation to the stand-
> ards for the award of QTS, with an assessment of their performance.
>
> (DfEE 2000a: para. 4)

In relation to planning and reviewing the NQT's support programme, induction tutors need:

- full access to, and knowledge of, the school's policies and procedures; a clear picture of how induction fits into the wider context of teachers' professional development,
- to be familiar with the standards for the award of Qualified Teacher Status,
- a thorough understanding of the Induction Standards and the require-ments for satisfactory completion of induction,
- an ability to work with the NQT to set, use and review appropriate development objectives,
- a knowledge of the resources available to support NQTs both within and beyond the school.

(TTA 2001b: 6)

A primary coordinator reported that the programme was 'totally and utterly tailored to the objectives and the action plan ... everything from that first meeting with the CEP, setting objectives and action plan'. The programme was planned to meet short, medium and long-term objectives.

A primary induction tutor planned the programme from her analysis of NQTs' initial needs. She made sure she covered the important areas relat-ing to the induction standards. Courses were identified and the NQTs met with all the curriculum coordinators, the SENCO and staff from outside services. For instance, some NQTs were driven around the area by the school nurse who discussed outside agencies, and then gave them relevant documentation, which the induction tutor shared with the whole staff. The NQTs also undertook observations of experienced teachers modelling good practice, in their own school and then others. There were meetings on parents' evenings, classroom management and with the link inspector. Box 5.3 gives an example of an individual primary NQT programme.

A secondary induction tutor reported on working with one of her ex-NQTs for input into what makes a programme work from the NQTs' point of view: 'I want to find out for next term what A and X want from the course. They might have individual needs or they might collectively choose something.' She offers them a menu of possible activities such as classroom management, working with the industry links coordinator, the SENCO, the Key Stage 2 primary–secondary liaison officer.

An experienced induction coordinator in a school with particularly good practice in induction designed the programme in Table 5.3. It is

Table 5.3 An example of how a primary school organised induction programmes for three NQTs

| Week | NQT X | NQT Y | NQT Z |
|------|-------|-------|-------|
| | Initial meeting with induction tutor | | |
| Wk1 | Induction tutor and NQT – 0.5 day – to set objectives and action plans | | |
| Wk2 | 0.5 day with **** for assessment policy and procedures | 0.5 day with **** SENCO ICT coordinator | 0.25 day to observe **** 0.25 with induction tutor for issues raised |
| Wk3 | 0.25 day for observation planning | | |
| | 0.25 day with ****, Wed 27.9.00 9–10.30 SEN | | |
| | 0.25 day to observe numeracy lesson of experienced staff | 0.25 day to observe **** | 0.25 day to review **** |
| Wk4 | Induction tutor to observe NQTs. 0.25 day for debriefing/feedback | | |
| Wk5 | 0.5 day for LEA assessment course, Tuesday 10 Oct. | 0.25 meeting with school nurse to discuss outside agencies. 0.25 SEN with KS1 SENCO | 0.5 day to meet with KS1 SENCO |
| Wk6 | 0.5 day to review progress and objectives | | |
| | | 0.5 day for LEA course, classroom management, Tuesday 17 Oct. | 0.5 day for LEA course, classroom management Tuesday 17 Oct. |
| | Half term | | |
| Wk1 | 0.25 day for observation preparation | | |
| | 0.5 day to meet with KS2 SENCO | 0.5 day – LEA Early Years course, Tuesday 31 Oct. | 0.5 day LEA course on behaviour management |
| Wk2 | Induction tutor to observe NQTs. 0.25 day for debriefing/feedback | | |
| | 0.5 | 0.25 observation of Reception **** | continued |

*Table 5.3* Continued

| Week | NQT X | NQT Y | NQT Z |
|---|---|---|---|
| Wk3 | 0.5 used in week 1 | 0.25 day for observation of Reception 0.25 to meet **** N.SEN | 0.25 – School nurse |
| Wk4 | 0.25 Briefing music with ****. 0.25 NQT observe **** deliver year 4 lesson | 0.5 day – resources | 0.5 day – observe experienced staff member (Behaviour manage/curric. manage) PE KS1 |
| Wk5 | 0.5 used in week 2. 0.25 to observe **** (from week 5) | 0.5 used week 4. 0.25 – Meet **** – discuss Foundation stage music scheme | 0.25–Observation of **** 0.25 – Analysis of observation (Numeracy instead) |
| Wk6 | 0.5 day for meeting to review progress and objectives | | |
| | 0.25 SEN evaluation | 0.5 day – ARR | 0.5 – SEN, review and update |
| Wk7 | 0.5 day for Assessment meeting 1 IT and NQT. Focus: Consistency in meeting standards for QTS | | |
| Wk8 | 0.25 used in week 5 | 0.5 used in week 6 | 0.5 used in week 6 – SEN |

based on identified needs, in so far as it has been developed after the initial meetings with the NQTs, and it is individualised to each NQT with some activities common to all three. Although the schedule was published well in advance, the programme was responsive to change and amended when necessary. When each activity was conducted, it was ticked off.

## Meetings with NQTs

Induction tutors in some schools that we visited found it useful to record key points from the meetings they had with their NQTs. These provided a useful record and focused discussion. Copies were kept by both the induction tutor and NQT in induction files and provided evidence that procedures had been fully followed. Figures 5.1 and 5.2 are examples of formats used.

| RECORD OF INDUCTION MEETING | | | |
|---|---|---|---|
| TERM | | WEEK | |
| PARTICIPANTS: | | Date | |
| Agenda | | | |

| Content | Objectives/<br>Action to be taken | Date<br>completed |
|---|---|---|
| | | |

| Things generally<br>going well | General things<br>to improve | Progress with<br>Action Plan | Progress on<br>Current Objectives |
|---|---|---|---|
| | | | |

*Figure 5.1* A record of an induction meeting

| RECORD OF INDUCTION MEETING |
|---|
| Participants      Date & time |
| Agenda |
| Things that are going well |
| Things to improve |
| Progress on current objectives |
| Objectives and action plans<br>  – Short-term<br><br><br>  – Longer term |
| Date of next meeting |
| Focus of next meeting |
| Signatures |

Figure 5.2 A record of an induction meeting (Bubb 2000c: 66)

# Chapter 6

# How Appropriate Bodies work

Every school and college that provides statutory induction has to have a designated Appropriate Body. This will usually be the Local Education Authority (LEA) in England, but Jersey, Guernsey, the Isle of Man and Gibraltar are also Appropriate Bodies. Sixth form colleges have a choice of which LEA they work with. Independent schools can either negotiate for an LEA to play this role or choose the Independent Schools Council – Teacher Induction Panel (ISCTIP). This chapter considers Appropriate Bodies' statutory responsibilities and how they are carried out, and examines our research findings about their non-statutory role in providing courses for NQTs and induction tutors.

Appropriate Bodies have been put in place to support and monitor both the provision of induction by schools and colleges and the teaching standard of individual NQTs. They are a conduit for the termly assessment reports, and assist induction tutors and head teachers in making fair assessments of NQTs. Critically, they make the final decision on whether NQTs are meeting the induction standards and convey that information to the General Teaching Council. Thus, Appropriate Bodies have overall responsibility for ensuring the quality of induction. They provide a range of support, monitoring and assessment activities to raise the quality of NQTs' induction experience, their teaching performance and the implementation of induction by their schools.

## Statutory responsibilities

The induction circular outlines what is expected of Appropriate Bodies. Their specific statutory duties are:

1 ensuring that head teachers and governing bodies are aware of and capable of meeting their responsibilities for monitoring, support and guidance (para. 19). Ensuring head teachers are capable of undertaking a rigorous and fair assessment of NQTs (para. 19).
2 making the final decision about whether an NQT meets the standards

for the completion of the induction period and communicating their decision to NQTs, schools and the DfES/GTC (para. 87).

3    keeping records and assessment reports on NQTs (para. 21).
4    providing a named person for NQTs to contact if they are unhappy with schools' support, monitoring and assessment (para. 32).
5    extending the induction period in exceptional circumstances (para. 82).
6    ensuring that schools with NQTs get earmarked funding (para. 101).

(DfEE 2000a)

From 2001 to 2002, £5 million was allocated for Local Education Authorities to retain centrally for costs relating to assessment, monitoring and evaluation of the induction arrangements. This specific funding for the Appropriate Body role was brought in to ensure that LEAs fulfil their role following the discovery that 67 per cent of LEAs had not retained any money centrally for induction, in its first term, despite having significant responsibilities (NUT 2000a: 10). Many LEAs had devolved all the money to schools that was allowed for induction through the funding mechanism of the Standards Fund. At the time of writing LEAs have on average £3,333 for each year. One may question whether this is enough for them to carry out their significant responsibilities.

Across the country as a whole, within LEAs and amongst senior staff in schools, the funding and regulations have raised the status of induction. Only a small number (9 per cent) of schools and one or two LEAs had previously prioritised induction very highly. These therefore experienced a decrease in funding when induction became statutory.

Our research team investigated 60 per cent of all Appropriate Bodies in England and we concluded that they were carrying out all elements legally required of them. Many Appropriate Bodies give a considerable amount of extra support and so go well beyond the statutory guidelines, although a few work at a level much closer to the minimum legal requirement. The introduction of central government funding for induction has helped considerably.

## Failing NQTs

One of the Appropriate Bodies' key roles is to identify and help NQTs at risk of failing as early as possible. This gives them time to implement extra programmes of support. Identification of those in danger of not passing their induction period is the joint responsibility of schools and Appropriate Bodies. It tends to be done through:

*   induction tutors or head teachers contacting their Appropriate Body. This would normally be as soon as lesson observations and any other evidence suggested that an NQT was struggling to make progress.

- Appropriate Bodies observing the NQT teach during a routine monitoring visit to the school.

Making the decision to fail an NQT is very difficult. It is the Appropriate Body which makes the final decision, but this has to be based upon strong evidence from the school. Schools welcome advice and intervention on this matter.

Some Appropriate Bodies and schools work together to move an NQT to another school rather than fail them. An Appropriate Body representative remarked, 'You know what happens don't you? We get them to leave before they fail.' NQTs who have not made sufficient progress and are still seriously struggling to meet certain induction standards near the end of their three-term induction period are not allowed to be given extensions unless they have been absent for thirty days or more.

*Table 6.1* Examples of how Appropriate Bodies fulfil their statutory responsibilities

| Responsibilities | Examples of AB practice |
| --- | --- |
| Ensuring that head teachers and governing bodies are aware of and capable of meeting their responsibilities for monitoring, support and guidance. | Sending the induction circular and other documentation to heads and governing bodies. The audit in Table 6.2 is useful for this. |
| Ensuring head teachers are capable of undertaking rigorous and fair assessments of NQTs. | Training for induction tutors. Checking termly assessment forms. Quality assurance visits to agree judgements about NQTs. |
| Making the final decision about whether an NQT meets the standards for the completion of the induction period and communicating their decision to NQTs, schools and the DfES/GTC. | Quality assurance visits to agree judgements about NQTs. |
| Keeping records and assessment reports on NQTs. | Administrative work, but hampered by schools not returning forms. |
| Providing a named person for NQTs to contact if they are unhappy with schools' support, monitoring and assessment. | This is either the person with ultimate responsibility for induction in the AB or someone outside the support and assessment role, such as someone from the personnel dept. |
| Extending the induction period in exceptional circumstances. | This decision is taken by the person with overall responsibility on the advice of all concerned. |
| Ensuring that schools with NQTs get earmarked funding. | Sending funding termly. Some ABs only send the funding when assessment forms have been received. |

Table 6.2 An audit of school induction practice (based on TTA 1999a: 20–23)

| Components of the induction arrangements | Has been addressed | Is being addressed | Still to be addressed |
|---|---|---|---|
| **Continuity and progression** | | | |
| How familiar are key staff with: | | | |
| • the structure and purpose of the Career Entry Profile? | | | |
| • the standards for the award of QTS? | | | |
| • the induction standards? | | | |
| Do those involved in the induction process have access to copies of the standards for QTS and induction? | | | |
| **Monitoring and support** | | | |
| *The induction tutor* | | | |
| Has an appropriate colleague been identified as the induction tutor for each of the NQTs in your school? | | | |
| Do they already have the skills, expertise and knowledge they need to do the job effectively, or will they need additional preparation? | | | |
| *Targeted professional development activities* | | | |
| How will you ensure that the induction programme of each NQT in your school reflects both their individual needs and the specific teaching context? | | | |
| Is everyone involved in the induction arrangements confident that they can identify appropriate professional development activities, in and outside the school? | | | |
| How will the induction programme relate to wider school professional development activities? | | | |

## Monitoring and support

*Observation*

Is everyone involved in the induction arrangements confident in planning for focused observation of and by the NQT?

How will observations and their follow-up discussions be organised?

How will the outcomes of observations be recorded?

*Review discussions*

Is everyone involved in the induction arrangements confident that they understand the purpose of the professional reviews of progress, and the procedures for undertaking them?

Are those involved in induction confident that they can support NQTs to set and review objectives for professional development that are specific, manageable and achievable?

How will objectives and action plans be recorded?

How will the outcomes of reviews be recorded?

## Assessment

Is everyone involved in the induction arrangements confident that they can plan for and undertake fair, rigorous and well-founded assessments against the induction standards?

How will the evidence that will be needed for summative assessments be identified and recorded without creating unnecessary bureaucracy?

Do those involved in summative assessment need further preparation and training to undertake their responsibilities effectively?

Are the procedures for assessment clear to all involved, including the NQT?

Are induction tutors aware of the procedures to be followed in the event of an NQT experiencing difficulty?

## Roles and responsibilities

Is everyone involved in the induction arrangements clear about their roles and the responsibilities they are taking on?

Do they have access to the information and support they need?

Do any of them need specific preparation?

Is everyone aware of the role of the LEA and the named contact?

*continued*

Table 6.2 Continued

| Components of the induction arrangements | Has been addressed | Is being addressed | Still to be addressed |
|---|---|---|---|
| **Whole school approach to induction**<br>To what extent are the induction arrangements integrated into the school's wider professional development and performance management systems?<br>Is the wider school community aware of the school's plans for the new induction arrangements, and their responsibility for supporting new teachers? | | | |
| **Documentation**<br>Has the necessary documentation been prepared and collated for all those with key roles and responsibilities, including the NQT? | | | |
| **Quality assurance**<br>Has the school made provision to monitor and evaluate the quality of its induction arrangements?<br>Are you clear about how your LEA will liaise with you in discharging its quality assurance responsibilities?<br>What provision will be made for the NQT to raise any concerns about the induction programme? | | | |
| **Funding**<br>Are you clear about how the funding arrangements for induction apply to your school?<br>Are you confident that the funding is used appropriately? | | | |

Therefore, to maximise an NQT's chances, they are encouraged to move at the end of their third term to a different school. Moving NQTs rather than failing them raises a dilemma.

On the one hand it may:

- help the teacher shortage situation a little,
- mean that NQTs don't fail just because they are in challenging schools.

On the other hand:

- the newly employing school may not know the background of the NQT because references and induction paperwork aren't received before appointing,
- if it is 'shifting the problem elsewhere' then it is poor practice,
- it goes against the spirit of the induction regulations.

In both July 1999 and July 2000, the number of NQTs who were deemed to have failed their induction period was minimal. In 2000, only forty-five out of over 16,000 NQTs failed. However, there is no moderation between Appropriate Bodies to continue to ensure that criteria for failing NQTs are implemented uniformally across the country. For head teachers and induction tutors working with NQTs who are in potential danger of failing, Appropriate Bodies provide a sense of security. That is, they give LEAs external judgements of an NQT's performance against the induction standards. Appropriate Bodies can also advise on the evidence base needed in case an NQT appeals against the judgement.

To date, approximately 40 per cent of Appropriate Bodies have established formal procedures for dealing with potentially failing NQTs. One example is a staged approach:

1st    Identification of a potentially failing NQT by a school or an LEA inspector's observation.
2nd   Immediate allocation of an LEA adviser or advanced skills teacher to the case.
3rd    A diagnosis of the cause of the problem made to determine what action to take.
4th    Further support put into place.
5th    Close monitoring of progress by school and Appropriate Body.

At the other extreme was an Appropriate Body who said that they only made one extra classroom observation to confirm the school's judgements.

The trigger for higher than usual intervention by Appropriate Bodies was, for 25 per cent of the LEAs we surveyed, solely based on the end of term assessment reports. All Appropriate Bodies look at which judgement box has been ticked – whether progress indicates that the NQT will complete induction successfully or not. Appropriate Bodies which demonstrate best practice also check assessment forms for the first and second terms for:

- cross-referencing with induction standards
- the evidence base for judgements made.

Whilst over three-quarters of Appropriate Bodies read every single final assessment form, others only select a sample. At present, most Appropriate Bodies do not give feedback to schools on their termly and final assessment report forms.

It may be that an NQT is not making progress despite high-quality school induction provision. However, schools themselves may also be the reason why an NQT is seen to be struggling. This is why the Appropriate Body's monitoring of school provision for their NQTs is essential. This was an area very strongly commented upon by many of the 530 NQTs we surveyed.

Particularly problematic were LEAs that had weak relationships with local schools and/or markedly less rigorous monitoring procedures and policies than other LEAs. A member of Appropriate Body staff expressed concern over the quality of provision by a large minority of schools but felt that many obstacles were in the way of changing this situation. Examples include:

- getting schools to return paperwork such as their selection of courses and termly assessment forms was excessively time-consuming. Because this material was often not returned to the LEA, induction programme management and the targeting of needs were difficult.
- the prevailing attitude of some head teachers that it is counter-productive to take NQTs out of school for courses, so that the Appropriate Body did not meet NQTs at courses.
- some head teachers are obstructive to LEA intervention because they expect autonomy.
- schools have difficulty coming to terms with the new induction requirements.

Tighter monitoring of schools, to ensure induction is a quality experience for NQTs, appears to be an area that many Appropriate Bodies are currently working on. A new practice seems to be emerging in some of the Appropriate Bodies in our research, namely that they are withholding funding until the assessment form has been received. This has been instituted to strongly encourage all the schools which previously sent in forms late or not at all, to do so on time.

## Non-statutory responsibilities

As well as carrying out their statutory responsibilities of monitoring and assessment Appropriate Bodies can 'provide guidance, support and assistance to schools, and training for teachers on their role of providing induction training, supervision and assessment' (DfEE 2000a: para. 20). So, Appropriate Bodies do not have to offer support but they often do because they are jointly responsible with schools for the quality of provision and because schools generally welcome their input.

## How work is shared within the Appropriate Body

Induction tutors, head teachers and LEA staff can gain much from understanding how different Appropriate Bodies are organised. Box 6.1 illustrates some of the range of ways that LEAs deploy staff to fulfil the Appropriate Body role. One of the problems that they encounter is that there is rarely enough work to fund posts for induction alone so this role is almost always taken on in addition to other work.

Our research found that the turnover of personnel responsible for induction within LEAs is high. This is a concern because it takes time and experience to set up effective procedures and build relationships with schools. Appropriate Body staff found the following aspects of their work to be challenging.

1 Intense workload around the beginning of each academic year, particularly in getting details of all NQTs and to prepare programmes. Some schools do not inform the person with responsibility for induction in an LEA that they have an NQT, assuming that personnel departments will convey this.
2 Chasing up overdue assessment reports.
3 Delivering support programmes to small groups of non-September starters.
4 Dealing with assessment procedures for those who start induction mid-way through a term.
5 Constraints on the monitoring of induction due to the high numbers of NQTs and low numbers of LEA staff.
6 Dealing with groups which are effectively 'outside' the system, such as supply teaching NQTs or head teachers who resist LEA involvement.
7 Weak NQTs who take up a disproportionate amount of Appropriate Body time.
8 Organising the payment to schools of at least £1,000 per term per NQT.
9 Keeping track of those NQTs who leave or arrive in the LEA during the year.
10 Contacting previous schools and their Appropriate Bodies for assessment forms.

**LEA 1**

a    LEA inspector responsible for induction overall.

b    Administrative officer in charge of keeping records on NQTs, distributing the £1,000 a term, collecting assessment reports.

c    Members of the LEA advisory service observe most NQTs once during the year, as part of their general school monitoring role.

d    Induction Consultant to organise training programmes for NQTs and induction tutors, and to organise quality assurance visits to a third of the schools with the help of five Advanced Skills Teachers (ASTs).

e    Five ASTs to support NQTs or schools with induction-related problems one day a week. Assigned to a school one day a week for a term or half term.

f    Human resources officer is the 'named person' outside the support and assessment roles, to whom NQTs can turn if their school is not supporting them. She is rarely used, since the other people involved normally sort out problems.

*Comment:* this Appropriate Body works well because there is close contact between all parties – most share an open-plan office and all are in regular email contact. The LEA inspector with overall responsibility is very active.

**LEA 2**

a    Human Resources officer responsible for induction overall. With an administrator, in charge of keeping records on NQTs, distributes the £1,000 a term and collects assessment reports.

b    LEA inspector organises training programmes for NQTs and induction tutors.

c    Members of the LEA advisory service observe most NQTs once during the year, as part of their general school monitoring role.

d    Panel of head teachers evaluates the termly assessment forms and make decisions about who passes and who fails. They intervene in cases of failing NQTs or where disputes arise.

*Comment:* this Appropriate Body separates its quality assurance and assessment role very clearly from its support role. The people involved in each are in different buildings and have little contact with each other.

**LEA 3**

a    Administrative officer in charge of keeping records on NQTs, distributing the termly funding, collecting assessment reports.

b    LEA inspector responsible for induction but who has a caretaker role, rather than making strategic decisions.

c    Induction Consultant A to organise training programmes for primary NQTs and induction tutors.

d    Members of the LEA advisory service will keep an eye on NQTs during the year, as part of their general school monitoring role.

e    Induction Consultant B to visit all the NQTs and judge their school's induction provision twice a year.

f   Induction manager from a Beacon school to organise training programmes for secondary NQTs and induction tutors.

g   Management of Induction Group consisting of LEA inspector, head
teachers, induction managers and tutors, ex-NQTs from all sorts of
schools and a representative of a local training institution. They work as
an interest group. For instance, they successfully petitioned for induction tutor role funding.

*Comment:* this Appropriate Body devotes most resources to induction but
its effectiveness is hampered by poor communication and a lack of one
person actively in charge. There is duplication because people do not tell
each other what they are doing. The LEA inspector with overall responsibility is very active.

*Box 6.1* How three LEAs with approximately the same number of NQTs (120) staff the
Appropriate Body rolepolicy for term one (secondary)

Some Appropriate Bodies are proactive and others are more reactive.
Our research evidence indicates that induction tutors, head teachers and
NQTs prefer proactive Appropriate Bodies, and that they are more effective in all aspects of their role. Table 6.3 summarises the characteristics of
each.

Proactive Appropriate Bodies have systems which start in the term
before most NQTs start. For instance, in July many LEAs run a course
outlining the statutory requirements of induction for induction tutors and
head teachers. Our research found that everyone who attended a session
like this considered it highly effective, even essential. See Figure 6.3 for
the outline of one such course held in July to prepare schools for September. Systems need to be in place for schools to inform Appropriate Bodies
as soon as an NQT has been appointed. Staff are in contact with the LEA
recruitment officers who organise the LEA pool of NQT applicants and
who know which schools have vacancies that might be filled by new
teachers. See Figure 6.1 for an example of a form that gathers all the
information needed.

LEAs and other institutions publish the NQT and induction tutor
courses and network meetings in the summer term. This enables schools to
coordinate release time or free periods with the courses. Some LEAs'
NQT and induction tutor courses are accredited through a university.
Table 6.5 is an example of one LEA course for primary NQTs. It was held
on Thursday mornings and repeated in the afternoons to allow schools
flexibility, and to restrict numbers to about twenty-five per session. The
previous chapter contains an example of an induction tutor training programme (see Box 5.1).

*Table 6.3* Characteristics of proactive and reactive Appropriate Bodies

| Proactive approach | Reactive approach |
| --- | --- |
| Dialogue within and between all groups of participants is central.<br>*Example:* close relationships, learner-centred support programmes. | Communication between participants is limited.<br>*Example:* didactic courses; head teachers resisting LEA involvement; staff with different roles not knowing what each other are doing. |
| Preventative measures taken against poor induction experiences.<br>*Example:* visits to certain schools prioritised, feeding back to schools on assessment reports for future improvement. Surveys of NQTs. | Reactive measures when problems arise.<br>*Example:* Reliance on the school to notify the Appropriate Bodies of NQTs at risk of failing. |
| Multiple strategies employed by a team to address each of support, monitoring and assessment.<br>*Example:* support through courses, network groups, visits to schools and telephone/email. | Single strategies used by Appropriate Bodies with small staffing levels.<br>*Example:* contact letter to NQTs inviting them to attend courses, with no follow up. |
| Provision is continuous throughout the period and progression is made explicit.<br>*Example:* rationale of year-long programme is shared, support is appropriate to phase in induction, discussion of suitable future targets built in to feedback sessions. | Provision appears to NQTs as sporadic and uncoordinated.<br>*Example:* NQTs unclear about roles of LEA staff, agendas for visits not established in advance. |

Our research found that 14 per cent of schools have very little relationship with their Appropriate Body beyond the submission of termly assessment reports. Further, although the Appropriate Bodies we talked to were extremely clear about the need for an early and ongoing programme, this was not the perception of some NQTs. Coherence and cohesion rather than a 'bitty' experience was welcomed. Therefore, Appropriate Bodies need to make more explicit the progression that exists in their year-long structure of support and monitoring. Our research also indicates that those NQTs, head teachers and induction tutors who have a close working relationship are more satisfied with the overall process.

## Forms of monitoring

Appropriate Bodies monitor the quality of:

1  induction provision in schools,
2  assessment reports,
3  NQTs' teaching performance,
4  The Appropriate Body's systems.

A few Appropriate Bodies told us that whilst they have responsibility for induction, they have only limited powers to control what happens in schools. This means that Appropriate Bodies need to devise ways to encourage, guide and influence, rather than impose change. Several did this by publishing induction newsletters and sending out questionnaires. The latter was effective not only in providing a picture of provision in the area but in reminding people about all the elements of the induction entitlement.

All Appropriate Bodies visit at least some schools. Interestingly, we found that 40 per cent of Appropriate Bodies observe and give feedback to between 1 per cent and 24 per cent of NQTs and, at the other extreme, 38 per cent do so for between 75 per cent and 100 per cent of NQTs. So, Appropriate Bodies across England appear to follow distinctive policies and practices. The range of these is summarised in Table 6.4. Whilst some aim to see almost all NQTs, others are highly selective. It may be of interest to note that observations and feedback from the Appropriate Body are valued highly by all in school.

*Table 6.4* Levels of monitoring by Appropriate Bodies in schools

| | |
|---|---|
| Universal | Every NQT visited once, twice or three times per induction period. |
| Target certain schools | Schools with staff shortages, particularly challenging children or previous records of poor induction provision. Approximately 25 per cent of schools visited. |
| Target certain NQTs | Head teachers inform Appropriate Body or assessment forms indicate that an NQT is not making sufficient progress towards meeting the induction standards. |
| Universal once, then targeted | Observe every NQT in every school once. Select 20 per cent to visit again. Perhaps use link inspector's reports to monitor a further 20 per cent. |
| Only visit when requested by a school | Policy of a reactive Appropriate Body (see Table 6.3). Less than 5 per cent of NQTs visited. |

Typically LEA visits to schools include the following:

- look at induction paperwork. For each NQT this includes: the Career Entry Profile, objectives set, diary or list of activities carried out in the 10 per cent release time, notes from meetings with the induction tutor or other staff, lesson observation notes and assessment forms.
- talk to the NQTs (ten to fifteen minutes), using a questionnaire as a starting point. This is done with all the NQTs at the same time, or individually.
- talk to the induction tutors about how they manage their role (twenty minutes) using a questionnaire as a starting point.
- observe one NQT for between thirty and forty-five minutes. Views on the lesson will be feedback orally and briefly in writing.
- speak to the head teacher about strengths and weaknesses in the school's induction provision.

Appropriate Bodies are required by the induction circular to keep records to assist monitoring. Information is generally kept on a database. Figure 6.1 has an example of an initial information form. Many Appropriate Bodies encounter problems in trying to keep this data up to date.

## The named contact

NQTs have an active role in enhancing the quality of induction they receive. The induction circular states that all Appropriate Bodies must provide a 'named contact' for their NQTs, who plays no part in their assessment and to whom concerns not solved at school level can be raised. All Appropriate Bodies have indeed designated a named contact but just less than one-quarter use someone who is an assessor as well as a monitor of induction. Our research found that, in practice, NQTs rarely go to their 'named contact'. Rather, they go to the nearest LEA person at hand such as their link inspector or induction course leader. They tend to prefer someone they have met face-to-face rather than speaking to a stranger.

## How Appropriate Bodies fund their services

Earlier in this chapter we discussed the central government funding for Appropriate Bodies. It is a relatively small amount, which LEAs supplement by charging for services beyond those which are strictly statutory. There are two main systems that LEAs offer to schools – an induction support package or individual elements. We found that the former was more effective than the latter, in that it provided better value for money and gave LEAs more flexibility.

| NQT Information for the Appropriate Body | |
|---|---|
| Full name | |
| Home address | |
| Date of birth | |
| Date of appointment | |
| DfES number | |
| National Insurance number | |
| NQT induction course to be attended | |
| NQT's specialist subject | |
| Key stage | |
| Age range | |
| Year group taught during induction year | |
| Secondary: subject taught during induction year | |
| Part-time or full-time contract | |
| Permanent or temporary contract | |
| Teaching qualification | |
| ITT provider | |
| Date QTS awarded | |
| Date skills tests passed | |
| School name | |
| DfES number | |
| School induction tutor | |
| Induction tutor course attended | |

*Figure 6.1* An LEA NQT information form

### Induction support package

Schools pay between £150 and £500 per year to buy services from LEAs. Service level agreements are signed which may include a selection of or all of the following: observation and monitoring visits; access by telephone to Appropriate Body staff when needed; and NQT and induction tutor courses. One Appropriate Body described this system as insurance for schools against employing under-performing NQTs because they provide substantial extra support. Financing induction activities appears more secure in this model and provides equitable support across all participating schools.

---

**Preparing to have an NQT**
**July 14**

Course outline:
The structure of the induction period
Clarification of the responsibilities of NQTs, head teachers, induction tutors, governors and the LEA
The induction tutor's role in the support, monitoring and assessment of NQTs
The qualities of an effective induction tutor
The standards for the end of the induction year
Using the Career Entry Profile
Target setting
Setting up a school-based induction programme with the NQT
How to prepare your NQT before they start teaching
Feedback from national and LEA reviews of induction practice
Preview of NQT and induction tutor training planned

---

*Box 6.2* Example of a course preparing schools for their role in induction

*Table 6.5* An LEA primary induction programme

| Date | Focus |
| --- | --- |
| 20 September | Induction in the LEA. Meet key figures. Listen to an ex-NQT talking about her induction year. Relating to parents informally and at parents evening. |
| 11 October | Visit to Beacon school – two lesson observations focusing on classroom management. |
| 1 November | Behaviour management. Time management. |
| 8 November | Pupils with SEN and the very able. |
| 29 November | Literacy. Your assessment. |
| 17 January | Assessment and target setting |
| 31 January | Resources on the Internet. Pupils with English as an additional language. |
| 14 February | Pupils with emotional and behavioural difficulties. |
| 14 March | Science or music. Your assessment. |
| 2 May | Reporting to parents. ICT or PE. |
| 23 May | Numeracy. |
| 13 June | Your assessment. Preparing to be a subject leader. |

### School chooses individual elements

Schools devise their own programmes and buy what support they need when they need it. For instance, they will buy more LEA support if they have an NQT who is struggling. Individual elements are priced highly but the school saves money by not having to pay for services they do not need. In this system NQTs, head teachers and induction tutors tend to be acutely aware of costs allocated to individual courses and other services. This system hinders LEA planning since they are unable to predict what services will be bought.

## Courses for induction tutors and NQTs

Courses are run by a range of providers: LEAs, ISCTIP, universities and private training organisations. The experience of the large majority of induction tutors and NQTs is that certain courses – introduction to induction for both induction tutors and NQTs and behaviour management for NQTs – are extremely useful. Unfortunately, the rest are thought to be of variable quality. NQTs complain strongly about courses on aspects of teaching and learning as well as subject-based sessions for the following reasons:

- content covered during initial teacher education is repeated,
- sessions are badly run. Preparation, resourcing, presentation techniques and enthusiasm are weak,
- the different needs and starting points of participants are not recognised.

Delivering information to a large group works well for the introduction to induction sessions because participants want clear guidance. This is not the case with sessions on subject knowledge and teaching and learning. Individual needs tend to be so diverse that they are rarely met through large group sessions. Some schools send NQTs' targets to the course leader when the booking form is sent in. Course providers need to take more seriously the need for relevance to individuals' induction objectives. In general, NQTs do not like to be 'talked at', but want to discuss professional issues with fellow NQTs and engage in practical activities that can be tailored to their own context, as the following comments indicate:

> What I find most useful is ... when you get to mix with NQTs from other schools ... and share experiences ... When you have group activities to do, when you get up and you leave the pieces of paper and you exchange ideas. ... We want to be involved with other people who are at the same level as us, working out ideas.

Further, teachers expected lively, motivating presentations with attractive overhead projector slides and handouts. Particular criticism was made of courses that raised issues but did not offer a range of clearly defined solutions. These problems are not new – they have been highlighted by research for many years. The DfES publication *Good Value CPD* (2001) may go some way to address these problems.

So, what can school staff and course providers do to maximise the effectiveness of courses in the future? Course providers need to understand teachers' experiences to-date and need to monitor their courses more closely. Brief course evaluation forms are found to be of use but some more in-depth investigations could help. Box 6.3 may assist course providers clarify what our research found to be components of successful induction-related courses.

---

- Good communicators:
  - presenters of sessions are interesting to listen to, vary their teaching techniques and are motivating.
- Participant-centred content:
  - induction-specific courses are very clear on both statutory entitlements and expectations from the NQT and the school.
  - subject-based courses do not repeat that covered during Initial Teacher Education.
  - opportunities are built in for the sharing and problem-solving of issues being encountered.
  - it is clear how ideas can be applied back in the classroom.
- Apply local understanding:
  - the contexts of teaching found locally, such as teaching pupils with English as an additional language, are understood. Support and guidance consistently reflects this.
- Inform schools:
  - schools are informed about the content of sessions so that an NQT's learning can be supported and spread to whole school development, if appropriate.
  - knowledge of local schools is used to compile lists of 'best practice' teachers for NQTs to observe.
- Promote semi-structured networking:
  - networking sessions for induction tutors and NQTs are provided for support.

---

*Box 6.3* Features of successful induction courses

## Training for induction tutors

Training for induction tutors is distinctive and needs special attention. There are different types of support, preparation and guidance for induction tutors:

- single or multiple session course – induction tutor skills training,
- single session course – familiarisation with, and practical guidance on implementing statutory induction,
- telephone query line,
- email query and response,
- forwarding of induction documents – LEA packs, TTA supporting induction booklets and the DfES circular.

The proportion of induction tutors that attend training sessions varies. For example, a quarter of LEAs only get up to 25 per cent of schools represented whereas a further quarter get between 75 and 100 per cent.

A distinctive pattern emerged from what induction tutors liked about the different courses they went on and how useful they were:

- initial meetings at which the statutory requirements are outlined and expectations for the induction period made clear,
- feedback from the induction courses that their NQTs had attended,
- moderation workshops – to compare how their NQTs are doing,
- opportunities to share good practice on specific topics and ideas for school-based programmes,
- hearing experienced Appropriate Body personnel interpreting and mediating the TTA and DfES documents with a view to practical implementation, particularly highlighting the most essential elements,
- examples of completed forms for induction programmes, observation, assessment, etc.,
- sessions where teachers felt they became informed about an aspect of induction and then discussed its application in their own school contexts.

What was not favourably received were:

- information presented in ways that overwhelmed the attendees,
- poor presentation style,
- unrealistic expectations of what can be achieved by induction tutors.

## Networks

Network sessions were seen as highly effective for both induction tutors and NQTs. Some teachers find it difficult to justify networking themselves but, in the light of our research, we would encourage people to reassess this thinking. Attendance at network sessions is crucial because it gives opportunities for participants to share their own emotional, social and cognitive thinking with colleagues who can empathise directly. Or, as Peter Earley puts it, 'As numerous studies of NQTs ... have shown, if there is one thing that new teachers value highly it is the opportunity to meet with others in similar situations to themselves' (Earley 1996: 127). One NQT told us that networking relieved anxiety by understanding that she was not alone: 'It's not only me!' An induction tutor told us:

> To actually discuss issues with other induction tutors is incredibly helpful. It's this feeling that you would be on your own and hoping that you're making the right sort of decisions . . .

Earley goes on to discuss the 'affective domain'. This is a useful term to summarise all those elements of doing induction that are very important but which lie outside the practical meeting of objectives, lesson observations, etc.

Some induction tutors feel that they are paying less attention to the affective domain as a result of what they see as the bureaucratisation of induction. They consider that they are spending more time completing paperwork than supporting new teachers in the way they did before statutory induction. The lack of clear formats for recording work means that in some cases induction tutors are making induction more paper heavy than it needs to be, because they are worried about being accountable. Networking helps reassure people that they are doing a good enough job.

The other reason that networking is so important is that it is an effective learning mechanism. NQTs and induction tutors can bounce ideas off each other, discuss matters that are relevant to them and gain ideas of good practice. Dialogue is the key. By partially structuring sessions rather than leaving them totally unstructured, there is a relevant focus, a chair for large group discussions and for gathering resources.

LEAs are ideally placed to facilitate networks, but we found examples where people organised their own. In setting up or joining a network one needs to consider its purpose and format. Box 6.4 gives a range of options that are currently in operation around the country.

| | | |
|---|---|---|
| • | Entirely social gatherings | These provide emotional support and insights to the work of others in informal settings. |
| • | Moderation networks | Small groups brought together to enhance monitoring and assessment skills through moderating portfolios, assessment forms, etc. |
| • | Workshops | Usually task-based, semi-structured activities. |
| • | Surgeries | An induction tutor or NQT 'drops-in' to discuss issues with a member of Appropriate Body staff. |
| • | School 'cluster' group meetings | Often initiated by LEAs but then run for and by teachers. |
| • | Buddy systems | Pairs of induction tutors or NQTs who offer mutual support. |
| • | Email networks | No restriction on numbers or location of participants. Questions, answers, issues, etc., can be shared at any convenient time. |

*Box 6.4* Types of network

## Support for Appropriate Bodies

Staff in Appropriate Bodies are usually isolated from other induction colleagues around the country. Their work is specialised, so they are unlikely to get help with induction-related queries from within their organisation. The TTA have been active in responding to this problem. They have organised regional networks, linking LEAs, HEIs and schools, to share effective approaches to induction and to support consistency across the country. The TTA keeps a database of all people involved in induction at LEA, HEI and consultant level. There is also a closed part of the TTA website (www.canteach.gov.uk) specifically for LEA induction coordinators to share good practice and ask questions of the TTA induction team.

The TTA have organised several national conferences on induction, including one in 2001 to launch the Induction Tutor guidance. On 23 March 2000 the TTA and LGA jointly hosted a conference to provide colleagues from schools, LEAs and HEIs with an opportunity to reflect on the first two terms of implementing the statutory induction arrangements, and to share ideas about effective induction practice and how LEAs, ITT providers and schools could work more effectively together at local and regional levels. Over 300 delegates attended from schools, LEAs, ISCTIP, professional associations, ITT organisations, governors' associations and supply agencies.

In March 2000 the TTA conducted a survey of NQTs' views of their initial training. About 85 per cent rated the overall quality of their training as very good or good. Only 1 per cent rated it as poor. There was, however, variability in the ways in which the NQTs rated different aspects of their training. In particular, they rated less favourably the extent to which their training:

- prepared them for teaching pupils from minority ethnic groups,
- provided them with the knowledge, skills and understanding to use ICT in subject teaching,
- prepared them for the induction period, and
- prepared them to teach pupils of different abilities.

Such information is useful for people planning induction training courses, and for schools in considering useful objectives for NQTs. The latter is the subject of the next chapter.

# Chapter 7

# The Career Entry Profile and setting objectives

The foundation stone of induction is meant to be the Career Entry Profile (CEP). This chapter describes the CEP and how the TTA intends it to be used, gives examples of where we found it working well, and discusses why in many cases it proved to be the least useful component of induction. It will look at ways in which it is being used in setting and reviewing object-ives, and offer alternative ways of doing so.

## The purpose of the Career Entry Profile

All students leaving English training institutions after July 1997 have a Career Entry Profile (CEP). It is intended to help the transition from initial teacher training to a job in a school, by providing information about new teachers' strengths and priorities for further professional develop-ment as seen at the end of the training. It also requires new teachers to set objectives for professional development and develop an action plan for induction. As such, it should be the primary tool of the induction in that it helps induction tutors and NQTs:

- make the best use of the skills and abilities the NQT brings with them,
- use the Standards for the Award of QTS and the Induction Standards to build on the new teacher's achievements,
- devise a focused and individualised programme of professional devel-opment, which will improve the NQT's practice in areas identified for development during the induction period,
- recognise the importance of effective professional development from the earliest possible stage in the NQT's career, and consider the new teacher's longer-term professional development,
- make sustained and significant improvements in the quality of the new teacher's teaching in relation to the teacher's own objectives, the school's development plan, and local and national priorities.

(TTA 1999a)

Our research found, however, that in many schools it did not work well. NQTs and induction tutors considered it a 'dispensable rather than an essential dimension' and something that had not quite found its place in the system.

The CEP has three sections:

*Section A*
A summary of the NQT's initial teacher training, including any distinctive features of their training (completed by the ITT personal tutor and the NQT).

*Section B*
Summary of the NQT's strengths in four bullet points and four priorities for further professional development (agreed between the ITT provider and the NQT).

*Section C*
Action plan, including objectives, for the induction period (agreed between the school and the NQT).

## How the CEP is completed

Our research found that the usefulness of the CEP depended greatly on how it was completed. It was usually seen as tacked on to the end of a training course rather than an 'organic' part of the training process. Many NQTs completed it in a rush at the end of the year and were unsure of how honest they should be. It was described as being like a reference in celebrating strengths, but people were wary of writing their weaknesses – and then did not know what to do about them.

The worst university practice found was where strengths and areas for development had to be chosen from a bank of statements. These were broad, not individualised and had no relevance to the Foundation Stage curriculum. For instance, an NQT who knew she was going to be teaching a reception class had to choose this as an area for development:

> More secure knowledge of the structures, concepts, content and principles of the National Curriculum programmes of study for geography across KS1 or KS2; increased personal knowledge and understanding of geography and how to teach it in primary schools.

Other poor practice was exhibited by universities which told their students to write only two areas of development rather than four. Many areas for development were either too vague (such as 'A level'), bland, written in meaningless educational jargon or 'written for a whole cohort of people'. This sort of practice is potentially damaging since it can set NQTs off on an unhelpful course. The TTA produced more detailed guidance for training providers in 2001 but we found no evidence that this had improved the quality and effectiveness of CEPs.

At best NQTs filled the CEPs in with a tutor after detailed discussion about their final teaching practice:

> I had definite aims. . . . It's like the last bit that I haven't quite done. It was something to keep me on track.

Induction tutors wanted the CEP to act as an up-to-date reference:

> It works better when it's not just a self-audit but it represents in fact an outsider's perspective from the training provider.

## NQTs sharing the CEP with their school

The CEP is completed at the end of a teacher training course, normally by the university tutor and student, and is sent to the student's home address after QTS has been awarded by the DfES. NQTs should have it in order to share it with the school as soon as they take up employment. Even this proved problematic. Fourteen per cent of each of the 1999–2000 and 2000–2001 cohorts of NQTs did not discuss their Career Entry Profile with their school. One must wonder why such a large number of NQTs did not, since this is one of their responsibilities.

The CEP is meant to start the whole induction process off. We found that 20 per cent of NQTs had discussed their CEP with the school, usually with their induction tutor, 'before the start of the first term' and 64 per cent did so 'at the start of the first term'. However, 8 per cent only did so 'later in the school year', which is worrying since sharing it after the start of the first term defeats its purpose. Some NQTs reported a delay in receiving the profile for the following reasons:

- qualified teacher status was delayed because skills tests or written work had not been passed,
- universities insisted that all debts were settled before granting the qualification,
- it was lost in the post – particularly common where the NQT had changed addresses.

This delay hinders the intended good early start. The induction tutor is responsible for supporting the NQT and helping to implement a programme of monitoring, support and review based on the action plan set out in the Career Entry Profile.

It is important to analyse the Career Entry Profile carefully and seek clarification from the NQT or training institution of any areas of confusion. The information about the training course is very important. The geographical area of the institution may also give important clues to the sort of schools and pupils the student came across on teaching practice. This will also alert schools to NQTs who are new to the area, with all the problems that entails. We found that induction tutors rarely read the Notes of Guidance that formed part of the CEP since this belonged to the NQT and few tutors had their own copy. This reduced the potential effectiveness of the CEP.

## Analysing areas of strength and priorities for further professional development

At the end of their course the beginning teacher and their tutor should agree four areas of strength and four areas where further development would be beneficial in relation to the standards for Qualified Teacher Status. These might refer to particular strengths in subject knowledge; planning, teaching and class management; assessment; and professionalism. Judgements will usually be made on the basis of the last teaching practice. The breadth of the areas of strength may give insight into how well the last teaching practice went.

Once in school, the induction tutor and NQT need to consider the statements made in Sections A and B of the profile, and look at them in the light of:

- the particular knowledge, understanding and skills needed to perform effectively in their specific teaching post,
- meeting the induction standards,
- their aims for their longer-term professional development. Many NQTs are happy just to be teaching a class of their own, but others have a clear career plan. For instance, the NQT may want to become an English coordinator or educational psychologist and so would want to be gaining experience that would be useful.

We found many cases where the CEP quickly lost relevance and thus failed to fulfil its potential as a reflective development tool, being regarded by many NQTs as unnecessary extra paperwork. This was sometimes the result of the CEP having low status in school and induction tutors not knowing quite what to do with it. It was not always seen as the keystone of induction, as these NQTs' comments illustrate:

It's one of those documents that you hand to your induction coordinator on your first day and you don't see again ... There was a lot of fuss made over getting this document right for something that I haven't seen since September ...

I didn't find it as useful as I'd thought it would be. It's very hard to know what your targets are going to be when you're in your teacher training school because of lots that you need to change when you come to a different school.

I soon found that things I was concerned about before I started teaching were no longer a concern.

Our findings corroborate those of other researchers in the field. McLeod found that the introduction of the induction year 'has done nothing to improve the somewhat patchy nature of this provision' and that 'providers and potential users lacked a shared understanding as to its purpose' (McLeod 2000: 43). The OFSTED research reported that only a half of secondary and one-third of primary schools found the NQTs' Career Entry Profiles from their initial training to be useful as an initial pointer to training needs and as a recording device. The FEFC research into the implementation of induction in sixth form colleges found that 'most' NQTs provided their college with their CEP but that the quality of the CEPs was considered generally inadequate by almost all colleges and NQTs (FEFC 2001: 14).

## Using the Career Entry Profile to set objectives for the induction period

Once induction tutors have analysed the NQT's strengths and areas for further development from their course, they need to think about the most useful objectives that will help the NQT to be a successful teacher in their school. Section C of the CEP (see Figure 7.1), the objectives and action plan, is at the core of the statutory induction arrangements for NQTs. The objectives set for each NQT should be individual, and relate to the induction standards, the areas of strength and priorities for further professional development identified at the end of training, and the demands of their first post.

The first set of objectives should be agreed as soon as possible after the NQT is in the post so that they can be shared with all those involved in supporting the NQT. These need to be decided in discussion with the NQT and be based ideally on an observation of teaching, looking at plans, assessments and other documentation, and looking at the classroom. They will not automatically be the same as the ITT priorities for development. For instance, some Career Entry Profiles highlight the need for input on music but if this is taught by a specialist in the school it would not necessarily need to be covered.

We found that only 77 per cent of respondents used the CEP to set objectives. Slightly more primary NQTs had done so than those in secondary schools.

| Targets | Actions to be taken and by whom | Success criteria | Resources | Target date for achievement | Review date |
|---|---|---|---|---|---|
| To improve management of pupil behaviour | Strictly control entry/exit to classroom. Continue to develop a more assertive manner with pupils. Move around classroom to monitor pupils' work and behaviour. Continue to develop higher profile when dealing with pupil misconduct. Observe good practice by other teachers with classes causing concern. Further INSET on behaviour management. | Ground rules for conduct are adhered to by pupils. Uses praise and encouragement. Pupils dealt with herself and contacts made with parents. Improving pupil–teacher relations seen in formal observations and elsewhere. | Cover for observation of more experienced colleagues (two periods). Further course on classroom management and discipline. | Spring half term | End of Spring Term |

| To develop ICT skills within the MFL curriculum. | Develop awareness of existing potential for use of ICT in MFL by consulting with Mr D. Find out about use of 'Fun With Text' package on network via Mr M. | Meetings undertaken with Dn and Mt. Lesson plans/ observations show evidence of ICT. | Use of non-contact time for meeting. Cover for observation of ICT in another dept (two periods). | End of February | End of Spring Term |
|---|---|---|---|---|---|
| To gain experience in A-level teaching and assessment | Read and absorb OCR syllabus (Gd). Observe A-level lessons (Gd). Take on responsibility for delivery and assessment of an A-level topic (Gd). | Has overview of A-level course. Follow-up evaluation of observation. Successfully plans and delivers topic. | Possible need for cover for observation (two periods). Delivery of topic via teacher-swap of lessons. | End of May | End of Summer Term |

Figure 7.1 Targets for an MFL teacher using the CEP format

Many schools found that NQTs were used to setting themselves objectives from their training and that in this they had an advantage over others
in the profession. Others felt that NQTs and induction tutors needed a
great deal more guidance in setting objectives and drawing up action
plans, in order for them to be most effective in aiding progress.

Schools varied in the degree to which they helped NQTs meet their
objectives. Some left NQTs to meet them without giving any support.
Others were very supportive:

> We have a commitment to help them reach those targets by providing
> appropriate development. Now that might be internally or it might be
> by sending people on appropriate courses.

The system of setting objectives was described by an induction tutor as
'proactive':

> Now we're saying make sure you make the most of your targets
> because it's going to drive your professional development.

## Good practice in setting objectives

The TTA guidance about setting objectives makes the useful point that
some NQTs

> may find it difficult to distinguish between objectives, which identify
> what they intend to achieve, and the supporting action plan, which
> describes what needs to happen in order to achieve the desired
> outcome.
>
> (TTA 2001c: 11)

Where objectives were most effective, they were SMART:

- Specific,
- Measurable,
- Achievable,
- Realistic and relevant,
- Time-bound.

We found objectives such as 'Improve subject knowledge in English',
'Improve control', 'Improve planning', were too unspecific and all-
encompassing. The research showed that NQTs needed specific, well-
drafted objectives, which avoided induction tutor's own idiosyncratic
emphases and were clearly related to helping NQTs to improve the quality
of learning of their pupils. Properly drafted objectives are also clearly
related to the induction standards – the criteria upon which the teacher

will be judged. Where objectives were not related in this way they were unhelpful.

NQTs should have no more than three objectives at a time. It is encouraging for the NQT if at least one objective is to develop a strength. It is important that teachers feel ownership of the objectives. They should therefore be jointly negotiated, with the teacher being proactive about identifying areas to develop, and how they can be achieved. We found some bad practice such as induction tutors writing objectives with no input, or even understanding, from the NQT. Objectives still need to be set with successful NQTs. We found that many of the best new teachers were left to their own devices, but they too deserve to be challenged to make further progress.

## Ways to record objectives

Objectives should be recorded in the most useful and easy manner. The CEP has Section C for this and Figure 7.1 shows an example of how this format could be completed. Our research indicated that many NQTs did not physically write objectives in Annex C of the profile throughout the year, as is intended, saying that there was not enough space. OFSTED also found that it was not being used to chart progress across the three terms or to set targets (OFSTED 2001c: para. 32). One induction tutor was critical of the layout of the CEP:

> The way that it's laid out it doesn't seem to be part of something that you can make into a coherent body of paperwork. It would be much better not being part of that book for a start.

This induction tutor suggested:

> It would be much better as part of a portfolio of observations and meeting notes and the assessment forms but all together with the target as well. The target setting gets lost ... and it's not part of the assessment that's going on ... If the targets are important then the recording of and the meeting of targets ought to be part of the assessment forms and it isn't.

Induction tutors were unsure whether to set objectives for the areas identified for development in the CEP or whether to address what they considered more pressing needs. Best practice appeared to combine the two:

> I think the most important thing is looking at the current situation for setting your objectives and your action plan, whilst bearing in mind the areas for development in the CEP.

There seemed to be two different sorts of objectives set: long-term ones based on the CEP and more specific ones set as a result of lesson observations. In some schools these were not related, and were written in different places. Induction tutors thought that the need to transfer objectives set on observation feedback sheets to the action plan section of the CEP was a waste of time. Many people did not record objectives in Section C of the CEP, saying that the forms were too small and did not provide them with room to write what was needed. This sometimes resulted in written objectives getting lost. Another complaint about the action plan section was that there was no room to record or review progress. Induction tutors were unsure whether they should sign the objectives and action plans when they set them or when they had been completed.

Some schools recorded objectives in alternative ways, such as in Figures 7.2 and 7.3.

| Objective | Success criteria | Other arrangements | Review date |
| --- | --- | --- | --- |
| 1 To begin to use ICT regularly in the classroom as a support to core subjects. | Develop task cards for children to use on rota basis in morning, which develop and support learning in ICT, Maths, English and Science. | | 8 Oct. |
| 2 To plan and teach PE lessons with a clear structure and health and safety guidelines. | Observe experienced colleague and develop clear plans which contain health and safety guidelines. | Planning with M for PE lessons. | 8 Oct. |
| 3 To develop a manageable system for whole class assessment in core subjects. | Working assessment files in place for Maths, English and Science. | | 8 Oct. |
| 4 To plan for the support role in core subjects, using different strategies following advice from INSET. | Follow up discussion from observation by deputy head and plans to be checked by deputy head. | INSET by deputy head. Observation by deputy head. | 8 Oct. |

*Figure 7.2* An alternative way of recording objectives for a primary NQT

*Name:* Jenny          *Date:* 1 Nov.     *Date objective to be met:* 16 Dec.

*Objective:* To improve control, particularly after playtimes, in independent literacy activities, at tidying-up time, and home-time.

| Success criteria | Actions | When | Progress |
|---|---|---|---|
| Gets attention more quickly | Brainstorm attention-getting devices. Use triangle, etc., to get attention. | 4.11 | 7.11 Triangle made chn more noisy – try cymbal. |
| Rarely shouts | Voice management course. Project the voice. Don't talk over children. | 19.11 | 23.11 Using more range in voice – working! |
| Plans for behaviour management | Glean ideas from other teachers through discussion and observation. Watch videos on behaviour management strategies. Write notes for behaviour management on plans. | 4.11 | 12.11 Improvement thro lots of tips, staying calm and being more positive. Not perfect and exhausting but better. |
| Successful procedures for sorting out disputes after playtimes | Glean ideas from other teachers. Ask playground supervisors to note serious incidents. Children to post messages in incident box. | 11.11 | 18.11 Incident box really working for those who can write and I can now tell when there's a serious problem. |
| Successful procedures for tidying | Discuss what other teachers do. Start tidying earlier and time it with reward for beating record. Sanctions for the lazy. | 18.11 | 25.11 Sandtimer for tidying working well tho still a few chn not helping. Might try minutes off playtime. |
| Successful procedures for home-time | Discuss ideas with other teachers. Monitors to organise things to take home. Start home-time procedures earlier and time them (with rewards?). | 25.11 | 2.12 Changed routine so tidy earlier. Some Y6 chn helping give out things to take home. |
| Children succeed in independent literacy activities | Ideas from literacy coordinator. Change seating for groups. Differentiate work. Discuss with additional adults. | 2.12 | 9.12 All class doing same independent activity working better. Mrs H helping. |

*Figure 7.3* An action plan to meet an objective (based on Bubb 2001a: 35)

## Review

Objectives should be set throughout the year and develop to ensure that the NQT's needs are met and that the induction standards are covered. Box 7.1 shows a primary NQT's objectives that were set every half term.

## Ways to monitor objectives

Progress towards meeting objectives should be monitored to ensure that the NQT stays on course. Much of this can be done through informal dialogue but Table 7.1 shows forms of evidence that can be gathered during the year related specifically to the induction standards. Planning can be monitored using a format such as in Table 7.2. Table 7.3 is a proforma that is used for judging teaching through monitoring pupils' work in a secondary school. A teacher's overall assessment practices can be monitored using a format such as Table 7.4.

---

**1st half of Autumn Term**
To organise the classroom to ensure effective learning
To improve behaviour management

**2nd half of Autumn Term**
Increase pace in lesson introductions
To plan for pupils of different attainment, especially those with SEN

**1st half of Spring Term**
To improve procedures for assessment to inform planning
To develop target-setting in English and mathematics

**2nd half of Spring Term**
To make assessments more efficiently
To develop target-setting in science

**1st half of Summer Term**
To carry out Key Stage 1 tests on the class
To decide what level each child is working at in English, mathematics and science

**2nd half of Summer Term**
To write clear and informative reports for parents
To conduct parents' evening confidently
To plan an outing

---

*Box 7.1* An example of how objectives develop over the year

*Table 7.1* Ways to monitor an NQT's progress against the induction standards (Bubb 2000: 75)

| Induction standard | Forms of evidence |
|---|---|
| (a) Sets clear targets for improvement of pupils' achievement, monitors pupils' progress towards those targets and uses appropriate teaching strategies in the light of this, including, where appropriate, in relation to literacy, numeracy and other school targets. | Planning Assessment file Observation Pupils' work |
| (b) Plans effectively to ensure that pupils have the opportunity to meet their potential, notwithstanding differences of race and gender, and taking account of the needs of pupils who are: <br> • underachieving; <br> • very able; <br> • not yet fluent in English; <br> making use of relevant information and specialist help where available. | Planning Observation Pupils' work Special needs assistants |
| (c) Secures a good standard of pupil behaviour in the classroom through establishing appropriate rules and high expectations of discipline which pupils respect, acting to pre-empt and deal with inappropriate behaviour in the context of the behaviour policy of the school. | Observation Display of class rules |
| (d) Plans effectively, where applicable, to meet the needs of pupils with Special Educational Needs and, in collaboration with the SENCO, makes an appropriate contribution to the preparation, implementation, monitoring and review of Individual Education Plans. | Planning Assessment file Observation IEPs Pupils' work Discussion with SENCO & SNA |
| (e) Takes account of ethnic and cultural diversity to enrich the curriculum and raise achievement. | Planning Observation Looking at the classroom |
| (f) Recognises the level that a pupil is achieving and makes accurate assessments, independently, against attainment targets, where applicable, and performance levels associated with other tests or qualifications relevant to the subject(s) or phase(s) taught. | Assessment file Agreement trialling |
| (g) Liaises effectively with pupils' parents/carers through informative oral and written reports on pupils' progress and achievements, discussing appropriate objectives, and encouraging them to support their children's learning, behaviour and progress. | Reports Letters to parents Notes from parents' evenings |
| (h) Where applicable, deploys support staff and other adults effectively in the classroom, involving them, where appropriate, in the planning and management of pupils' learning. | Planning Observation Discussion with support staff |

*continued*

*Table 7.1* Continued

| Induction standard | Forms of evidence |
| --- | --- |
| (i) Takes responsibility for implementing school policies and practices, including those dealing with bullying and racial harassment. | Informal observation in lessons and around the school and playground |
| (j) Takes responsibility for their own professional development, setting objectives for improvements, and taking action to keep up to date with research and developments in pedagogy and in the subjects they teach. | Discussion Self-reflection Behaviour in meetings |

*Table 7.2* Monitoring a teacher's planning (Bubb and Hoare 2001: 75)

| Prompts | Comments |
| --- | --- |
| Is the planning organised suitably? Are the plans covering the appropriate parts of the curriculum? Is the teacher following the school planning policies and practices? Is the teacher following the school schemes of work and long-term plans? Are useful links made between subjects, to aid children's learning? Is the planning covering the same work as parallel classes? Does the planning show appropriate expectations? Has the teacher drawn up a realistic timetable for when different work is to be done? Are learning intentions clear? Are there different learning objectives and/or activities to allow children of different attainment to make progress? Does the planning take into account the needs of pupils who are not yet fluent in English? Do the activities enable objectives to be met? Are the resources and activities appropriate and interesting? Are there planned assessment opportunities? Are plans informed by assessing children's knowledge, skills and understanding? Are lessons evaluated? | |

*Table 7.3* Monitoring pupils' work – a format from a secondary school

Year Group & subject:

Timespan:                                                                 Comments
  1  Does the work have: date, title, aim/objectives?
  2  Use of departmental and whole college policies?
  3  Is the work related to teacher's planning, SOW and statutory
     requirements?
  4  Is it well organised and presented, with appropriate use of
     equipment?
  5  What does the work tell you about the student's motivation
     and concentration?
  6  Are activities varied and balanced?
  7  Is there unnecessary repetition of work?
  8  Differentiation – evidence of support/extension work and do
     tasks reflect the ability of the student – appropriate quality
     and quantity?
  9  Regular homework?
 10  Is there a difference between the work at the beginning,
     middle and end of books?
 11  Are there repeated errors by the student?

Marking and assessment – regular marking
 12  Use of departmental and whole college policies (e.g. literacy)?
 13  Evidence of praise and rewards (e.g. merits)?
 14  Are errors corrected or indicated?
 15  Are there strategies for repeated errors?
 16  Varied marking methods including involvement of students?
 17  Acknowledgement of: effort, presentation, attainment, NC
     level, GCSE grade, GNVQ grade, other (please indicate)?
 18  Clear, helpful, encouraging and positive feedback to inform
     students about their progress, and suggestions for
     improvement (formative assessment) and targets?
 19  Different types of assessment: formative, summative,
     continuous, informal, other(s) (please specify)?
 20  Evidence/impression of high expectations of teacher, and
     student motivation?

*Concluding summary statement:*

Signature of evaluator:

Table 7.4 Monitoring a teacher's assessment practices (Bubb and Hoare 2001: 96)

| Prompts | Comments |
| --- | --- |
| Are assessments organised suitably? | |
| Are assessments covering appropriate parts of the curriculum? | |
| Is the teacher following the school planning policies and practices? | |
| Are assessments analytical, rather than just descriptive? | |
| Is assessment information used to inform planning? | |
| Are pupils with SEN being monitored against their IEP objectives? | |
| Are appropriate objectives being set? | |
| Is progress towards the children's objectives being monitored? | |
| Is the teacher accurate in judging the National Curriculum level of pieces of work? | |
| Are record-keeping systems efficient? | |
| Is marking up to date? | |
| Is work marked against the learning intention? | |
| Are pupils clear about how well they are doing? | |
| Do they know what to do to improve? | |
| Are literacy and numeracy errors highlighted in all subjects? | |
| Are reports well written? | |
| Do reports give a clear picture of the child? | |

## Reviewing objectives

Professional review meetings should take place every half term to ensure that there is a dialogue about the NQT's progress, to celebrate achievements and to alert them to any problems. However, our research found that this did not happen for many NQTs, particularly after the first term. Some NQTs said that meetings were unnecessary since there was a continual dialogue about progress, but others had no feedback on how they were doing until the end of term report.

Review meetings should draw on evidence such as lesson observation, planning, pupils' work and NQTs' evaluations. Box 7.2 shows how the reviewing of objectives can be recorded.

## Professional Development Portfolio

One of the problems with the present system of documenting elements of induction is the lack of an integrated means of recording and storing assess-

*Objective One* – Kate has used level descriptors to assess children's attainment in science for those aspects of the QCA Scheme of Work already taught. She has prepared for teacher assessment at the end of Year 2 SATs, but is aware that these assessments may need further updating. She still needs to develop the use of assessment techniques and opportunities in PE and ICT.

She has worked with the KS1 Assistant Head teacher in devising a statement bank to report on individual attainment within history.

*Objective Two* – Kate has met all the success criteria identified and continues to strengthen her understanding of individual learning needs and styles and appropriate ways to respond.

*Objective Three* – Kate has met the success criteria this term, but as behaviour management is still an area she would like to develop further this target will be revised and extended.

*Objective Four* – again Kate has met the success criteria for the development of her subject knowledge in science, although the development of teaching AT1 needs further reinforcement. Geography will be the focus of her work in the summer term.

*Objective Five* – Kate has begun to identify learning objectives more independently but still needs to tighten up this aspect of her practice and ensure that all activities are driven by specific learning intentions.

**Revised objectives**
*Objective One* – to plan for and carry out formative and summative assessments for: PE, D&T, ICT, music and aspects of art.

To produce informative annual reports on individual children.

To carry out end of KS1 SATs.

*Objective Two* – NEW – to enhance classroom organisation and promote independent learning.

*Objective Three* – to enhance behaviour management and control in a range of settings.

To continue to give children choices regarding their own behaviour, but be more consistent when applying consequences to the selection of 'wrong' choices.

*Objective Four* – to extend subject knowledge and develop skill in teaching geography curriculum outlined in QCA scheme of work.

To look at the progression of skills development within music and deliver more effective lessons.

*Objective Five* – ongoing.

To remain focused on the target group during literacy and numeracy sessions.

*Box 7.2* An example of how objectives can be reviewed and progress recognised (TTA 2001: 21)

ment material. There is no folder or file where all documentation can be kept. This results in inefficient copying out of objectives from lesson observations, for instance, from one format to another. We recommend the use of a Professional Development Portfolio to contain key documents from training, which can be built up through the whole of a teacher's career. This fits well with the thinking behind the current DfES Continuing Professional Development (CPD) strategy and incorporates the idea of a Professional Development Record, which all teachers are recommended to keep (DfES 2001b). An example of material that may go in it is shown in Box 7.3.

The next chapter will examine issues concerning the reduced timetable, what NQTs, induction tutors and Appropriate Bodies found to be useful ways to spend this additional time, and whether this helped objectives to be met.

---

**Contents**
1. CV – Career history
   References
   Job description
   Qualifications
   The Career Entry Profile – containing information about the course undertaken and strengths and areas for development from initial training

2. Professional development
   List of courses and INSET attended
   Certificates from courses attended
   Other teachers observed
   Articles read
   Websites visited
   Reflection on how ideas gained from professional development have been implemented in the classroom

3. The school-based induction programme
   Diary sheets for planning and recording induction activities
   Notes from induction tutor meetings

4. Objectives
   Action plans
   Reviews of progress

5. Monitoring of your teaching
   Feedback on planning
   Feedback from lesson observations
   Feedback on pupil assessments and reports

6. The termly assessment reports

7. The school induction policy and induction circular

---

*Box 7.3* The professional portfolio

# Chapter 8

# The reduced timetable and how it is used

NQTs are entitled to a 10 per cent reduction in timetable. This is enshrined not only in the induction circular but also in the School Teachers' Pay and Conditions of Employment which sets out head teachers' responsibility to ensure that 'inductees' do not teach more than 90 per cent of a normal teaching timetable (DfEE 2000c: para. 138). NQTs in our research considered the 10 per cent reduction in teaching time to be the most important and valuable part of their entitlement.

This chapter considers our key finding that 20 per cent of NQTs did not receive their reduced timetable throughout the year. It discusses the DfES and TTA guidance on how the time freed by the reduced teaching timetable should be organised and used, and shares our findings about how it is being planned for and used. We look at the activities that NQTs find most useful.

## Provision of release time

One of the key findings from our research was that 20 per cent of NQTs did not get the reduced timetable at all times. This confirms the findings of other research. OFSTED found that only two-thirds of secondary schools had allocated their NQTs a timetable of no more than 90 per cent of the normal teaching time (OFSTED 2001c: para. 28). In a third of secondary schools the release time was inconsistent. Some NQTs had the target teaching load while others in the same school had a considerably higher teaching commitment. OFSTED found that almost all primary schools had allocated a reduced timetable but as the induction year progressed the teaching load increased so that 'about one-fifth' ended up with a teaching load in excess of the target (ibid.).

The issues relating to the release time are different in primary and secondary schools, with the 10 per cent reduced timetable organised differently. In primary schools, teachers normally work a 100 per cent timetable, so that the 10 per cent reduction is easy to see. In secondary schools, the

10 per cent is harder to identify because teachers have free periods, the numbers of which can vary between departments.

There are two main issues that both primary and secondary schools need to consider when deciding how to organise their reduced teaching timetable:

- how the 10 per cent will be distributed through the induction year,
- how to cover it to minimise disruption to pupils and maximise its benefits for the NQT.

There is a range of ways to organise the reduced timetable, as illustrated in Table 8.1. Primary schools usually timetable NQTs to be out of their class-room a half day a week and secondary schools allocate more free periods. One of the problems with the latter model is that free periods were not identified for being for induction. They were indistinguishable from others, and so were used simply to catch up on marking and preparation, rather than on induction activities. Problems also occur when NQTs join a school after the timetable has been drawn up, as the NQT will have to be provided with cover to be out of classes and clearly this disrupts pupils' learning. Some NQTs in all phases preferred having a whole day off as it gave them a chance to completely 'switch off'. The NUT suggest that any time given for release time should consist of at least half a day in order to be effectively used (NUT 2001a: 1).

### How the 10 per cent is distributed through the induction year

The induction circular states that the reduced timetable should be distributed evenly throughout the year. Our research found difficulties in this in

*Table 8.1* Ways to organise the reduced timetable

| Way organised | Comment |
| --- | --- |
| A regular half day each week | Most popular in primary schools |
| A regular day a fortnight | Second most popular in primaries |
| Twenty random days a year taken from full timetable | |
| 10 per cent fewer lessons timetabled | Most common in secondary schools |
| Twenty days a year, most of which are taken during exams | Popular in sixth form colleges |
| Combinations, e.g. a regular half day each week for two terms, then seven random days to be used in the third term | |

the first year of statutory induction, that became resolved when funding and regulations became clearer, as the following figures show:

- 67 per cent of the 1999–2000 NQT cohort had the reduced timetable distributed evenly throughout the induction year,
- 92 per cent of the 2000–2001 cohort had the reduced timetable distributed evenly throughout the induction year.

In schools where release time was not distributed evenly it was used as and when required or requested by the NQT. Some NQTs in our research favoured this flexibility as it meant that they could plan ahead for activities. Some training needs, such as visiting other schools, may require a whole day or longer. For example, if there was a two-day course, they could 'bank' release time for this. One NQT found that having release time 'blocked' in the school enabled them to get to grips with objectives and professional development in a systematic manner. Some schools identified half a morning release time each week and 'banked' the rest towards activities that took the NQTs out of the school.

Schools can alter the distribution of release time throughout the induction year to suit a particular NQT. In some schools the time was distributed evenly for the first two terms, then used more flexibly in the third term, to enable NQTs to conduct activities such as visits and courses outside the school. Some NQTs alternated between having half a day a week and a whole day a fortnight for release time during the induction year.

Head teachers should ensure that the reduced teaching timetable is addressed early in the planning of an NQT's induction programme to ensure that the NQT is supported throughout their induction year (TTA 1999b: 29; DfEE 2000a: para. 55). In some schools release time was not organised until well after the beginning of the induction year. The reduced teaching timetable should also continue to the end of the induction year, but we found that some NQTs in our research had reverted to a full teaching timetable in their third term. OFSTED found that about one-fifth of primary NQTs ended up with a teaching load in excess of the target (OFSTED 2001c: para. 28). NQTs highlighted the need for the 10 per cent release time to be organised throughout the year, as without it, they said, they carried a huge burden.

### Which mechanism(s) of cover to use

Schools in our research used a range of mechanisms to cover the NQT's reduced timetable. Many schools made decisions based on both minimising disruption to pupils' learning and maximising the benefit to the NQT. Some, however, emphasised one to the detriment of the other. For

Table 8.2 How cover for release time is organised

| Type of cover | Definition(s) | State (%) | Independent (%) | Sixth form (%) | Special (%) |
|---|---|---|---|---|---|
| Supply teachers | Short, medium or long-term supply teachers. | 42 | 0 | 14 | 39 |
| Enhanced staffing | Part-time staff are employed specifically to cover NQTs' classes. | 34 | 9 | 42 | 22 |
| Existing staff | Existing staff provide cover. | 22 | 82 | 29 | 39 |
| Outside classtime only | Meetings/activities only take place outside teaching time, such as during exams. | 1 | 9 | 29 | 0 |
| N of specific responses | | 232 | 33 | 14 | 18 |

Note
These figures are based on a different number of responses, see N. More than one answer could be given.

instance, one school released the NQT on Friday afternoons, which made it hard for them to benefit from observing other classes.

Schools either used regular or random supply teachers, part-time staff or existing staff to cover the NQTs' release time. Table 8.2 clearly shows variations between the four types of school surveyed. State schools were most likely to use supply teachers while 82 per cent of independent schools used their existing staffs' allocation of non-contact time. Seven respondents (39 per cent) in special schools said they used existing staff to cover lessons and the same number chose supply teachers. Some state schools reported 'splitting' or 'doubling up' classes. In primary schools head teachers were more likely to cover the lessons of NQTs than those in secondary schools.

### Supply teachers

The effectiveness of supply teachers taking class(es) for 10 per cent of the year was an issue for some respondents in our research. Some NQTs felt that there were times when they would have preferred to stay in the classroom. This was due to problems with having classes taught by supply teachers, such as:

- it was disruptive for pupils,
- they were unfamiliar with pupils and schemes of work,
- there was no opportunity to liaise with the supply teacher,
- they taught things badly, causing the NQT to have to teach lessons again.

Certain measures can be taken to reduce these problems. If possible the same person should cover NQTs' classes in order to maintain some kind of regularity for pupils. This would also give NQTs the chance to build a rapport with the supply teacher and opportunities to liaise with the teacher covering their classes.

## Was release time provided?

A large number of NQTs did not receive their basic entitlement of release time. Our research found that, in 1999–2000, 20 per cent of NQTs and, in 2000–2001, 19 per cent of NQTs had not received their release time throughout the induction year.

Five main reasons were given by schools in our research as to why NQTs were not receiving their release time:

- NQTs' free periods had been used to cover for absent colleagues in secondary schools,
- people allocated to teach primary NQTs' classes were used to cover classes of absent colleagues,
- there were no supply teachers available for NQTs' classes,
- some supply agencies charged so much that the £1,000 a term funding did not cover a reduced timetable throughout the year,
- some CTCs and independent schools claimed that they had no money for the reduced timetable.

The reduced timetable should not be dependent on levels of staff attendance or absence and the subsequent use of NQTs for cover. It should be protected. Some schools said that they only used NQTs for cover if they could not avoid it, but others seemed to exploit the inexperienced teachers' reluctance to object. In order to solve the problem of NQTs being used for cover, we consider that schools should:

- Protect free periods designated for induction.
- Structure the use of release time: where NQTs had arranged to do certain activities, release time was less likely to be cancelled. As one head teacher put it, if it is not structured at the beginning of the year other things 'take over'.
- Only use NQTs for cover as a last resort.

- Guarantee NQTs protection from cover in the first term, even if this is not possible in the second and third term.
- Reschedule any missed release time. If release time is missed due to staff absence, then it should be made up at a later date. Schools are delegated money to cover the 10 per cent reduced timetable and not for other staffs' sick leave. To ensure release time is rescheduled both the NQT and the school should keep a record of when it is missed.

### Lack of supply cover for NQTs

The precise cost of a supply teacher per day varies considerably between types of school and within schools. Our research found that for the year of 2000–2001 the price of supply teachers ranged from:

- £50 to £193 in state schools,
- £100 to £267 in independent schools,
- £110 to £147 in sixth form colleges,
- £100 to £166 in special schools.

Due to the general staffing shortages in the period covered by our research, 2000–2001, there were not enough supply teachers to cover all NQTs' classes. Some respondents said that, in particular, they could not get a supply teacher for just one lesson or a half day. Money was no good to them when they could not get teachers to actually come into the school.

**Case study**
One possible solution to supply teachers and their associated problems is to follow the example of a school that had vacancies for three NQTs. They knew that it would be difficult to find good quality supply teachers for three NQTs' classes and so they employed a fourth NQT which enabled them to release an experienced teacher for half a week. This person became the induction tutor who gained a very good picture of the NQT's progress by covering their release time.

It is the responsibility of the head teacher to provide NQTs with a way of raising concerns in relation to induction and making sure that these concerns are addressed satisfactorily (TTA 1999a: 31). If NQTs do not receive their full entitlement of release time then they are responsible for raising their concerns. Initially the NQT should follow their own school's procedures for raising concerns, which all NQTs should have been made aware of by the school (TTA 2001a). If the concerns of the NQT go beyond their school's systems, or if they feel that the school has not addressed their concerns, then the NQT should alert their named contact in their Appropriate Body (see Chapter 4). This had a beneficial effect in the case study below.

**Case study**
A secondary school NQT did not have a Head of Department and was not getting her reduced timetable. She made an appointment to talk to the head teacher and told him about her concerns. This did not resolve the issue and so the NQT spoke to someone from the LEA. The link inspector then intervened and ensured that her timetable was reorganised and that she got more support.

## How the 10 per cent can be used

The time released by the reduced teaching load may be used in whatever way is most appropriate to the needs of individual NQTs and their school (DfEE 2000a: para. 55). It is important to ensure that the time is not simply used as 'non-contact' time for routine planning or marking. It should be part of a coherent induction programme and used in order to enable NQTs to meet the induction standards (TTA 1999b: 28).

The extent to which schools ensured that release time was spent on induction activities varied considerably in our research. The importance of a year long programme of induction provision for release time was evident in the results of our NQT questionnaire. The respondents of our two NQT cohort questionnaires were asked whether they had a programme of activities and the results are shown in Table 8.3. In both cohorts, about a quarter said that they had had no activities during their induction year, suggesting that they were either not receiving release time or were using it simply as general 'non-contact' time.

*Table 8.3* Have you had a programme of activities to do in your release time?

| Programme of activities | % NQTs in 1999–2000 | % NQTs in 2000–2001 |
|---|---|---|
| Year long | 29 | 24 |
| Occasional | 38 | 49 |
| None | 30 | 24 |
| Other | 2 | 3 |
| Total (N) | 242 | 302 |

Source: *PEIY NQTs questionnaire; IOE.*

Note:
Due to rounding and non-responses percentages/figures may not sum to 100/N across columns.
This figures are based on a different number of responses, see N.

NQTs were asked to rate the effective use of their release time for induction activities on a four-point scale. There was a strong positive correlation between the effectiveness of use of release time and the level of provision of activities in release time:

- teachers who stated that their release time was used either 'very effectively' or 'effectively' had programmes of activities lasting throughout the year,
- teachers who stated that they used their release time either 'effectively' or 'quite ineffectively' only had occasional activities provided,
- teachers who considered that they used their release time either 'quite ineffectively' or 'ineffectively' had no activities provided.

It is clear that, the higher the level of provision, the more effective the use of release time is. This exemplifies how important it is for NQTs to have a programme of induction activities throughout the year.

Some NQTs in our research described how they had organised their induction activities alone. For example, one NQT had not had a Head of Department to guide her and so felt they had made the wrong choices, choosing generic courses rather than specialist ones. Others felt their release time might have been used more 'constructively' if someone had told them how to spend it.

Ideally the time should be used to meet objectives and action plans. A calendar sheet (Figure 8.1) can be used to plan and record what NQTs do in the time freed by the reduced timetable. It shows the link between activities and objectives, and also how school INSET and induction tutor meetings can contribute to a new teacher's development.

## Activities conducted during release time

NQTs can carry out a range of induction activities, such as:

1 reflecting on progress so far,
2 attending induction and other courses,
3 observing other teachers in the school,
4 observing teachers in other schools,
5 observing someone teach your class(es),
6 observing someone teach a lesson that you have planned,
7 observing how pupils of different ages learn,
8 looking at resources in the school, such as computer programs,
9 visiting local education centres, museums and venues for outings,
10 arranging a school outing,
11 looking at the educational possibilities of the local environment,

**Oliver's Autumn first half-term Induction Programme**

*Objectives:* To organise the classroom to ensure effective learning
To improve behaviour management
To gain confidence in relating to parents

| *Week beginning observation of NQT* | *NQT release time for induction* | *Induction tutor meetings* | *Staff, department meetings and INSET* |
|---|---|---|---|
| 6 September | 10 Sept LEA induction programme – The Standards. Relating to parents | The Career Entry Profile | Key stage 3 strategy training |
| 13 September | Organise room Label resources | Classroom organisation | Key stage 3 strategy training |
| 20 September Observation focusing on organisation and control | Observe Y7 focusing on organisation and behaviour management. | Feedback and discussion following observation | Planning |
| 27 September | 29 Sept LEA induction programme – classroom management Written reflection | Behaviour management | Parents evening arrangements |
| 4 October | Prepare for parents' evening Display | Parents' evening tips | Numeracy assessment |
| 11 October | Observe own Y8 class being taught by supply teacher Written reflection | Monitor planning | Review behaviour policy |
| 18 October | Observe Y9 Written reflection | Review of the half term objectives Set new objectives | Review behaviour policy |

*Figure 8.1* A calendar sheet to plan and record how release time is used on activities that enable objectives to be met (based on Bubb 2001a: 97)

12 working with the SENCO on writing Individual Education Plans (IEPs),

13 reading pupils' previous records and reports,

14 making some in-depth assessments of individual pupils,

15 improving subject knowledge through reading, observation, discussion, etc.,

16 analysing planning systems in order to improve their own,

17 analysing marking and record-keeping systems in order to improve their own,

18 standardisation meetings,

19 writing reports,

20 planning a lesson based on the thorough assessment of pieces of work.

21 making resources and displaying work,

22 learning more about strategies for teaching the pupils with special educational needs in their class,

23 learning more about strategies for teaching pupils with English as an additional language,

24 learning more about strategies for teaching very able pupils,

25 meeting with parents and preparing for parents' evenings,

26 meeting with outside agencies, e.g. social workers, speech therapists, educational psychologists, etc.,

27 updating the induction file and completing documentation,

28 discussing lesson observations,

29 meeting with the induction tutor and other staff.

Release time was used by NQTs as a breathing space and opportunity for reflection. They also used it to catch up on tasks such as planning and marking, which they felt took them longer than experienced staff. Research by both OFSTED and Bubb, however, found that release time was being overused for marking and preparation rather than induction activities (OFSTED 2001c: 2; Bubb 2000b: 4).

## Cost effectiveness and usefulness of induction activities

In our research, head teachers, induction tutors and Appropriate Bodies were asked how cost effective they consider various induction activities, whilst NQTs were asked how useful they found them. Our results are in Table 8.4. Lesson observations of all kinds were found to be the most cost effective and useful.

It is interesting to note the percentages of NQTs who had not conducted certain activities. For instance:

• 14 per cent had not observed anyone teach in their school,

• 29 per cent had not worked with the SENCO, in spite of induction

*Table 8.4* NQTs in 2000–2001 cohort perceptions of the usefulness of induction activities

| Activity | Perception of usefulness for induction | | | | |
| --- | --- | --- | --- | --- | --- |
| | Very useful | Quite useful | Not very useful | Not at all useful | Never done |
| Being observed with feedback | 53 | 36 | 7 | 2 | 2 |
| Meeting with your Induction Tutor or teacher | 39 | 43 | 11 | 5 | 2 |
| Discussing lessons observed with a teacher | 43 | 35 | 12 | 4 | 5 |
| Observing a teacher from your own school teach their own class | 46 | 31 | 7 | 2 | 14 |
| Doing pupil assessments and target-setting | 29 | 50 | 11 | 1 | 8 |
| Improving planning | 31 | 46 | 12 | 1 | 9 |
| Writing reports | 36 | 40 | 13 | 3 | 6 |
| Improving subject knowledge | 32 | 41 | 9 | 3 | 13 |
| Exploring resources | 34 | 39 | 10 | 1 | 14 |
| Preparing for parents meetings | 30 | 42 | 16 | 3 | 7 |
| Making resources and displaying work | 32 | 38 | 15 | 4 | 10 |
| Improving marking | 28 | 41 | 14 | 3 | 12 |
| Attending NQT sessions run by your LEA, an HEI or other organisation | 18 | 41 | 20 | 10 | 11 |
| Working with your SENCO | 23 | 34 | 12 | 2 | 29 |
| Observing someone teaching your own class | 18 | 16 | 3 | 1 | 61 |
| Observing teachers in other schools | 21 | 14 | 3 | 0 | 61 |

standard D requiring them to do so in order to make an appropriate contribution to individual education plans,
• 61 per cent had not seen someone teach their class but, those who had, found it useful,
• 77 per cent of secondary school teachers, but only 45 per cent of primary school teachers, had not observed in other schools.

These would appear to be missed opportunities.

Of all the activities, attending induction courses was the least popular, with 30 per cent saying they were not very or not at all useful. This is discussed at greater length in Chapter 6.

### Lesson observation

The most cost effective and useful activity is lesson observation of all kinds. All the NQTs we interviewed found observing others very helpful. However, there was a wide variation in the number of observations that NQTs carried out. Nine per cent of NQTs in cohort 2000–2001 had not observed any other teachers. This seems a significant missed opportunity. Table 8.5 shows that the frequency of observations of other teachers did not improve with time.

Lesson observations of other teachers have great value for NQTs' development as effective teachers. One induction tutor said that 'the NQTs have probably observed more staff this year than some people who have been here for six or seven years'. Our research found that most respondents conducted between three and five observations of other teachers. However, it seems a disappointingly small number, considering the NQTs' opportunity to benefit from such a valuable resource.

One induction coordinator speaks of the importance of NQTs observing experienced teachers teaching, as a way to individualise support, but points out that this needs training.

> First they have a chance to think about their own practice with the induction tutor. It sometimes takes a practised eye to see something straight away anyway. If they're not used to talking about lessons and thinking about them then they're not always clear about what they're looking for anyway.

The practice of these observations and the discussion with the induction tutor provides a useful model and with this individualised approach progression can be built in:

Table 8.5 Number of observations of other teachers' lessons made by NQTs

| Number of observations conducted | % of NQT cohort 1999–2000 | % of NQT cohort 2000–2001 |
| --- | --- | --- |
| 0 | 5 | 9 |
| 1–5 | 66 | 67 |
| 6–10 | 21 | 18 |
| 11–15 | 6 | 4 |
| 16–20 | 0 | 1 |
| 21–25 | 1 | 1 |
| Non-response | 1 | 0 |

In the first two terms we will spend time observing them, talking to them about their practice, giving feedback and so on, then gradually more during the second and third term they then start moving out and watching other teachers teach.

Other schools build in observation of other teachers in the first term, too. NQTs benefited greatly from seeing an experienced teacher teach their class, but this kind of activity is not fully exploited in schools.

Interestingly lesson observation of teachers in other schools was much more highly rated by primary than by secondary NQTs (32 per cent of primary NQTs rated it 'very useful', compared to 9 per cent of secondary NQTs). In a large school, with a variety of practice, there may not be the same need to go outside the school as in a smaller establishment. However, those who visited other schools, particularly those with Beacon status, felt it very worthwhile. A highly rated aspect of one LEA's induction programme was a group (25) visit to two Beacon schools. This took place in October when NQTs were looking at classroom management. They were given a simple format to note down points and consider what they could implement in their classroom (see Figure 8.2).

It is useful to have a focus for the observation, ideally linked to the NQT's objectives. Once it has been decided what is to be observed, it must be arranged. Induction tutors' support will lend weight to the request. Schools should ensure that adequate time is put aside to make observations, and that opportunities to talk about the lesson are scheduled so that the NQT can ask questions and discuss why certain strategies were used.

To gain the most from observing another teacher, we found that:

- a focus should be decided upon, related to something the NQT wants to improve,
- NQTs need access to the teacher's plans,
- notes should be made on a lesson observation sheet, paying particular attention to the effect of the teacher on pupils' behaviour and learning (see Figure 8.3),
- while observing, NQTs should try not to teach but concentrate on the teaching and learning.

School                          Teacher                          Year group

| Arrangement of the room | What and when implemented |
|---|---|
| Resources | |
| Behaviour management | |
| Teaching strategies | |

Figure 8.2 Observing other teachers – what have you learned? What could you implement in your classroom?

| Teacher | | Date and time |
| Subject | | Additional adults |
| Learning objective | | Observer |
| **Prompts** | **OK** | **Comments: what has the teacher done to get this response from the children?** |
| Pay attention | | |
| Behave well | | |
| Relate well to adults and pupils | | |
| Are interested | | |
| Understand what to do | | |
| Understand why they're doing an activity | | |
| Gain new knowledge, skills | | |
| Speak and listen well | | |
| Have errors corrected | | |
| Work hard | | |
| Act responsibly | | |
| Understand how well they have done | | |
| Understand how they can improve | | |
| Enjoy the lesson | | |

*Figure 8.3* Lesson Observation Sheet – how well children learn (Bubb 2001a: 90)

## Informal meetings with induction tutor and school staff

All meetings, other than review and assessment meetings, came next in ranked order as most cost effective and were rated as 'very useful' or 'useful' by 80 per cent. This underlines how important it is for NQTs to have the opportunities for meetings. Schools with a developmental culture, an open and enquiring stance on educational issues and where communication is good between staff, are viewed as providing a very good 'value for money' induction environment.

The lowest rated activity in terms of cost effectiveness and usefulness were the courses provided by consultants, or HEIs. Appropriate Body courses scored slightly higher in this rating. One NQT described her LEA NQT conference as:

> a complete and utter waste of time and waste of the funding provided for us. Given the cost of the course and the cover costs that's our money gone.

However, other NQTs really valued their LEA induction programme. When asked to evaluate how the programme helped them be a better teacher, some primary NQTs wrote:

> It has given me more confidence and extended my college training.

> Every session has had a number of things that have helped, mainly introducing new ideas and providing opportunity for group discussion. The support of other NQTs is also a great help.

Primary courses were more popular than those for secondary NQTs. This is because of the difficulty of running general courses for teachers of many different subjects.

### Timing of induction activities

During their first year of teaching, NQTs go through different stages, as outlined in Table 8.6. Initially many NQTs are simply trying to survive in the classroom and need quick tips and fixes. Therefore, courses and support regarding classroom management need to be accessed early in the first term.

### Time for reflective practice

The findings of our research raise the question: 'What constitutes an induction activity?' Release time should be used to support progress

Table 8.6 Stages that NQTs go through (Bubb 2000c: 13)

| | |
|---|---|
| Early idealism | Feeling that everything is possible and having a strong picture of how they want to teach: 'I'll never shout at a child.' They imagine children hanging on their every word. |
| Survival | The NQT lives from day to day, needing quick fixes and tips. They find it hard to solve problems because there are so many of them. Behaviour management is of particular concern – they have nightmares about losing control. They are too stressed and busy to reflect. Colds and sore throats plague them. Survival often characterises the first term, especially in the run up to Christmas. |
| Recognising difficulties | They can see problems more clearly. They can identify difficulties and think of solutions because there is some space in their lives. They move forward. This stage is aided considerably by a skilled induction tutor. |
| Hitting the plateau | Key problems, such as behaviour management and organisation, have been solved so they feel things are going well. They feel they are mastering teaching. They begin to enjoy it and don't find it too hard. But they don't want to tackle anything different, or take on any radical new initiatives. If forced they will pay lip service to new developments. Some teachers spend the rest of their career at this stage. |
| Moving on | They are ready for further challenges. They want to try out different styles of teaching, new age groups, take on further roles in the school. If their present school doesn't offer them sufficient challenge they will apply for a new job. |

towards the standards. Induction activities should be ones that help NQTs meet objectives and the induction standards and contribute to professional development.

Some NQTs saw release time as an important opportunity for reflection and self-evaluation, whilst away from the classroom environment. It was also described as important in terms of preventing NQTs from becoming too 'bogged down' or 'burdened', and allowing them 'breathing space'. Similarly, evidence from head teachers and induction tutors suggests that schools view the 10 per cent release time as essential because of the added 'planning and thinking time' needed.

So much of the normal school and classroom routines are new to the NQT that any activity such as assessing pupils' work, lesson planning and marking, could be described as induction activities if they are conducted as part of an objective and are reflected upon. Release time may provide the opportunity that Bleach and others argue must exist for critical self-reflection by teachers to occur (Bleach 2000: 143).

One way of ensuring that activities conducted are reflected upon is through keeping a record (see Table 8.7).

*Table 8.7* Reflection on induction activities

| Date/time | Activity | Purpose | Reflection |
|-----------|----------|---------|------------|
| 18 Jan | Assessment course | Improve asst and target setting | Lots of ideas. Need to prioritise time for work sampling that will lead to focused targets. |
| 24 Jan | Look at colleagues' assessment systems | To get ideas for manageable systems | Must try quicker, more focused marking using traffic light system and commenting on how well they've met learning objectives. |

Alternatively, NQTs may maintain a 'diary of reflection', keeping a record of activities conducted during release time. One NQT described their diary of reflection as 'probably the most useful tool for professional development'. It highlighted the things that went well and those that had not worked (Bleach 2000: 144). Reflection can also be conducted through dialogue between induction tutors and NQTs. This is particularly stimulated through discussion on specific aspects of teaching seen in a lesson. This is the subject of the next chapter.

# Chapter 9

# Observing NQTs

## Introduction

Lesson observation is one of the key mechanisms though which a beginning teacher can learn to improve practice. This fact was brought home to the research team when we questioned a range of professionals – induction tutors, newly qualified teachers, head teachers and personnel in local authority professional development roles – about what constituted effective induction practices. Eighty-nine per cent of NQTs found being observed very useful for their professional development, and induction tutors and head teachers found them to be the most cost effective of all induction activities. The huge proviso, which must be placed against these findings, is that lesson observation has to be carefully planned and accompanied by skilful professional dialogue between an accomplished practitioner and the new teacher. This role is usually taken by the induction tutor, although other members of staff and induction personnel will have an important part to play.

In this chapter we will consider observations made of the NQT's teaching by the induction tutor and other staff.

## The statutory regulations

Lesson observations of NQTs' teaching are a mandatory part of the assessment process, both formative and summative. The circular is very clear about the function which lesson observations should perform within the programme of support and training. It clearly defines when they should take place and lays down the process by which they should be made, including joint prior planning and post observation debriefing (DfEE 2000a: paras 47–49).

**How often should they take place?**
The NQT should be observed teaching at least once in any six to eight week period, i.e. once each half term, including in the first four weeks in post.

**What about an NQT working part-time?**
The induction period for a part-time NQT is calculated pro rata, so that the same number of school sessions is covered as for a full-time NQT (DfEE 2000a, para. 34). The intervals between observations should be adjusted accordingly, but the first observation should take place within the first four weeks.

**How should lesson observations be planned?**
Observations should focus on particular aspects of the NQT's teaching. The choice of focus for the observations should be informed by the requirements for the satisfactory completion of the induction period and by the NQT's objectives for development.

**What records should be made?**
A brief written record should be made on each occasion. This record should relate to the NQT's objectives for development and indicate where action should be taken. It should show any revision of objectives.

**Who should observe?**
The induction tutor is likely to undertake most of the observations. Other people from within or from outside the school may also be involved in observations: for example, teachers with particular specialism or responsibilities, Advanced Skills teachers, tutors from partnership Higher Education Institutes (HEIs), LEA advisers.

**How are lesson observations managed?**
Observations should be coordinated by the induction tutor.

**What about NQTs who are not making satisfactory progress?**
Early action should be taken in order to support and advise the NQT, and the head teacher is also required to conduct an observation of the NQT if they are not the induction tutor.

*Box 9.1* Regulations concerning lesson observations

## Our research findings

We found that being observed and receiving feedback on lessons was the most useful activity with 89 per cent of respondents describing it either as 'very useful' or 'useful'. The views of this NQT were typical:

> It's vital. It's just so informative having someone watch you teach because you can't see everything and sometimes you don't see what you do well, as well as the things you need to develop.

It was considered 'the most nerve wracking part but I think it's the most effective'. Many spoke of it as a positive and constructive experience. One NQT we interviewed said that she 'loved' being observed:

> I love showing my kids off as well ... I choose my lowest sets ... It raises their own self-esteem and it makes me feel really proud of them.

Induction guidance recommends that NQTs should be observed during their first four weeks of the induction period. One-quarter of our respondents were not. The reasons for this were:

- there were too many other things to do at the beginning of the school year,
- induction tutors thought that NQTs needed time to settle before being observed; this was often misplaced kindness,
- induction tutors did not know that they should do an early observation and were not yet trained to do so.

Eighty-three per cent of NQTs had been observed and given feedback at least twice in the autumn term, compared with 13 per cent who had not. During the spring and summer terms, the number of NQTs who had been observed twice each term and given feedback was slightly less than during the autumn term, namely 74 per cent. Thus, approximately a quarter of NQTs were not observed as often as the regulations require. A few respondents said that observations took place on the last day of term with no notice.

A variety of people observe NQTs teach: induction tutors, head teachers, mentors, heads of department, and representatives from the Appropriate Bodies. Some NQTs in our research found feedback from induction tutors more useful than from people outside the school. Others valued and were motivated by feedback from people they considered experts. One-third of NQTs were observed by LEA advisers or inspectors. For one NQT this was such a valuable experience that she described it as a turning point: 'He boosted my confidence immensely.'

## Good practice in observing

Principles of good lessons should underpin the work of the induction tutor and others who undertake lesson observations of NQTs. It may seem unnecessary at the outset to say that the observer should arrive before or at the start of a session, stay throughout and leave with the teacher at the end. Good classroom observation practice includes the following:

- negotiation with the NQT of the time and date well in advance, for the NQT to prepare,
- a focus for observation chosen in advance, negotiated between NQT and observer and related to developmental needs,
- an acceptable and appropriate method of recording observations, related to the focus chosen,
- helpful feedback that followed some basic principles such as those below.

Good feedback is:

- prompt – takes places as soon as possible after the lesson observation,
- accurate – based only on specific observations/evidence which can be readily shared with the NQT,
- balanced – the positive emphasised and points for development related to the focus chosen as an objective,
- respectful to NQT's perspective – allows for input from the NQT,
- related to objectives set for review and directly actionable by the NQT,
- it takes place in a quiet and private space.

The value of the dialogue which takes place when feedback is given after a lesson observation cannot be overemphasised. Its effect, however, depends on both the quality of the feedback and the relationship of trust between the observer and the NQT. As one primary NQT told us, reflecting on her own teaching through discussing a lesson observation was her most valuable learning experience:

> ... but I think that's only because I feel really safe with X and you feel that, you know she does have this credibility and it's only because of that relationship that you feel ... positive and encouraged.

A focus needs to be chosen in advance of the observation:

> There are certain things which we're trying to improve. So certainly they're helpful for observation, because then you've got a real focus, rather than just sort of observing out of the blue.

In our research we found instances where distinctions were made between the formal lesson observations relating to writing the reports at the end of the terms – summative assessment observations – and developmental observations. This distinction resulted in objectives being written in different places. Some schools reported an overly burdensome process of disassociating short-term objectives from long-term ones, copying them from one format into another, for example. Good practice suggests that *all* documentation relevant to induction should be kept in a Professional Development Portfolio, as described in Chapter 7 and Box 7.3.

## Lesson observation proformas

We found a variety of lesson observation recording sheets in our case study schools. Some schools use their own sheets, which related to performance management observations taking place for other staff. Some induction tutors found this a useful practice because they felt that it prepared their NQTs for life in 'the real word' of teaching and inducted them into the particularities of their own school context. For example, one secondary school was working on the behaviour management of disaffected boys, and had a category on the lesson observation forms to record strategies used to keep these pupils on task. A primary school's formats focused on literacy, since it was particularly concentrating on this area.

Other induction tutors thought that giving their NQTs performance management or lesson observations on an OFSTED type format was unfair, as it deprived them of the more individualised formats related to their needs. These induction tutors argue that induction review meetings take place each half term, whereas performance reviews for other teaching staff only take place once a year. They think that the recording process must therefore be based on different principles, relating to shorter-term objectives, formative assessment and feedback. One induction tutor wrote the objectives as headings for the observations and then made notes under them:

> I actually found that more useful than the observation form in [the official LEA Form] because that's too complicated, because it has to fit together with the official induction standards, so you have to keep cross-referencing the whole time, which you haven't necessarily got time to do in the middle of observing.

Some observation formats are subject-specific or focus on the teacher's movement around the class and interactions with different pupils. King's booklet has examples of both, relating to a geography classroom (King 2000: 27).

Induction tutors and local authority staff produce a range of recording sheets, some designed for general observation and others to suit the particular objectives chosen as a focus for development. A few of these are reproduced below (Figures 9.1–9.8). Box 9.2 contains one secondary school's supplementary list of features of effective teaching, for staff to use when observing any teacher. Possible areas for the post-observation discussion are shown in Box 9.3.

## Issues arising from lesson observation

All participants in our research were convinced of the crucial role lesson observation places in the development of NQTs. There are, however, some important issues.

### The time it takes

Induction tutors have difficulty finding time to undertake lesson observations:

> You end up using up all of your free periods for it ... There's the hour of the observation but then it obviously takes longer to then write up the feedback and then give the feedback. So that can end up being a significantly longer amount of time in that particular week.

One induction tutor calculated that an observation took at least two and a half hours:

- twenty minutes to plan it with the NQT and prepare for it,
- one hour to observe and make notes,
- forty minutes to reflect and write up a summary,
- thirty minutes for the post-observation discussion.

### The importance of feedback

The discussion after any lesson is essential in order for it to be worthwhile. This takes time, and skill that comes with training and experience. Box 9.3 has some good practice guidance.

### Observations from a range of people

Releasing other staff to do observations can be difficult, but it is important that the judgement about an NQT comes from more than one person. However, once a range of people are involved in observations there can be problems of consistency and a possibility of 'mixed messages' reaching the NQT. In some schools, observations of the same NQT carried out by the induction tutor, head teacher, other staff and LEA advisers gave different evidence of achievement. The most effective schools addressed this problem by having a consistent policy on observation for all staff.

### Bad practice

Bad practice in observing causes great problems and can damage the NQT's confidence. We encountered situations where the observer:

- arrived late and disrupted the lesson,
- observed without any notice,
- corrected the teacher's errors in front of pupils,
- looked bored or disapproving,
- did not give any feedback,
- gave written feedback without an opportunity for discussion,
- contradicted the views of the induction tutor,
- gave simplistic feedback without any ideas for further development,
- made erroneous judgements based on poor knowledge of the context,
- upset the NQT without giving positive ways forward.

The best practice schools avoided these faults by ensuring that all observations are carried out in accordance with school policies, which themselves drew on best practice.

### The cost

Lesson observations of NQTs, informal meetings and review and assessment meetings are hard to cost, because the time of induction personnel is given when required, and not strictly calculated on an hourly basis. Our research evidence suggests that time is given over and above the funding available. It is given willingly, but appears as a cost on teacher time and school resources. Nevertheless, the overall perception of most people interviewed matched this induction tutor who said:

> Get in to see your NQTs as soon as you can, because there's nothing that can compare with classroom observation.

In the next chapter we shall consider the assessment of NQTs. This draws largely on evidence from lesson observations.

## NQT INDUCTION
## LESSON OBSERVATION RECORD SHEET (TTA 1999b: 11–12)

| | |
|---|---|
| **Newly qualified teacher** | |
| **Induction tutor** | |
| **Class and subject/topic** | |
| **Date and time** | |
| **Focus of observation** | |

| Planning, teaching and class management | **Notes** |
|---|---|
| <ul><li>Sets clear targets for improvement of pupils' achievement, monitors pupils' progress towards those targets and uses appropriate teaching strategies in the light of this, including, where appropriate, in relation to literacy, numeracy and other school targets.</li><li>Plans effectively to ensure that pupils have the opportunity to meet their potential, notwithstanding differences of race and gender, and taking account of the needs of pupils who are:<br>  – underachieving,<br>  – very able,<br>  – not yet fluent in English,<br>making use of relevant information and specialist help where available.</li><li>Secures a good standard of pupil behaviour in the classroom through establishing appropriate rules and high expectations of discipline which pupils respect, acting to pre-empt and deal with inappropriate behaviour in the context of the behaviour policy of the school.</li><li>Plans effectively, where applicable, to meet the needs of pupils with Special Educational Needs and, in collaboration with the SENCO, makes an appropriate contribution to the preparation, implementation, monitoring and review of Individual Education Plans.</li></ul> | |

| | |
|---|---|
| • Takes account of ethnic and cultural diversity to enrich the curriculum and raise achievement.<br><br>**Monitoring, assessment, recording, reporting and accountability**<br>• Recognises the level that a pupil is achieving and makes accurate assessments, independently, against attainment targets, where applicable, and performance levels associated with other tests or qualifications relevant to the subject(s) or phase(s) taught.<br>• Liaises effectively with pupils' parents/carers through informative oral and written reports on pupils' progress and achievements, discussing appropriate targets, and encouraging them to support their children's learning, behaviour and progress.<br><br>**Other professional requirements**<br>• Where applicable, deploys support staff and other adults effectively in the classroom, involving them, where appropriate, in the planning and management of pupils' learning.<br>• Takes responsibility for implementing school policies and practices, including those dealing with bullying and racial harassment.<br>• Takes responsibility for their own professional development, setting objectives for improvements, and taking action to keep up to date with research and developments in pedagogy and in the subject(s) they teach. | |

*Figure 9.1* Lesson observation: in this example, the list of induction standards is used as an aide-memoire. This is helpful in keeping a focus on the criteria against which NQTs are to be judged, but they cover a vast area and some are unlikely to be evidenced in a lesson

| NQT INDUCTION<br>LESSON OBSERVATION RECORD SHEET (TTA 1999b: 13) ||
|---|---|
| **Newly qualified teacher** | |
| **Induction tutor** | |
| **Class and subject/topic** | |
| **Date and time** | |
| **Focus of observation** | |
| **Professional Development Objectives** | Notes |

Figure 9.2 Lesson observation: in this example, relevant objectives from the NQT's action plan are listed on the left-hand column to help organise notes taken during the course of the observation

| **Lesson Observation Sheet with prompts for looking at teaching (Bubb 2001a: 91)** | | |
|---|---|---|
| Observer | Obs started . . . ended . . . | |
| Teacher & Year group | | |
| Subject and learning objective | | |
| Prompts | OK | Comments and evidence: what impact does teaching have on pupils? |
| Planning<br>Groundrules<br>Praises good behaviour and work<br>Redirects off-task behaviour<br>High expectations<br>Organised<br>Resources<br>Shares learning objectives<br>Subject knowledge<br>Relate new learning to old<br>Explanations<br>Deals with misunderstandings<br>Voice<br>Pace<br>Use of time<br>Questioning<br>Motivating<br>Differentiation<br>Additional adults<br>Feedback to children<br>Suitable activities<br>Plenary | | Time: Pupils on task: . . . off task: . . .<br>Time: Pupils on task: . . . off task: . . . |

*Figure 9.3* Lesson observation: this sheet has prompts for looking at teaching and the impact on pupils. It has plenty of space to write in but useful prompts to tick or grade that remind the observer of the main aspects of teaching. It also allows the observer to record how many pupils were on task at two times in the lesson.

| Summary of Classroom Observation (Bubb 2001a: 92) | |
|---|---|
| Teacher | Subject, date and time |
| Observer | Focus of observation |
| Strengths of the lesson | |
| Areas for further development | |
| Objectives | |
| Teacher's signature and comment | |

*Figure 9.4* Lesson observation: this sheet is useful as a best copy summary of main strengths of the lesson and areas for development, allowing the sheet completed in the classroom (Figure 9.4) to be a note pad. The strengths would be completed after the observation during the essential reflection time and the areas for development and objectives would be written during the post observation discussion

| Name | Date | |
|---|---|---|
| **Class being observed** | **Observer** | |
| *Aspect of lesson* | *Present performance Grade 1–4 and comment* | *Other strategies* |
| Handling the entry and settling down | | |
| Beginning routines – register, starting instructions, returning work, etc. | | |
| Activities – appropriate number, sequenced, delivery | | |
| Handling transitions between activities | | |
| Getting attention to change activities | | |
| Having time at the end to discuss follow-up tasks | | |
| Endings and clearing up | | |

*Figure 9.5* Lesson observation: this form has a focus on pace throughout a lesson – an issue for many inexperienced teachers. It allows the observer to comment on parts of the lesson and suggest alternative strategies

| Name | Date | |
|---|---|---|
| **Class being observed** | **Observer** | |
| *Teacher initiated* | *Good points* | *Points to watch* |
| Welcoming pupils | | |
| Initial presentation and explanation of task(s) | | |
| Supervision of task(s) | | |
| Establishing expectations of behaviour during task | | |
| Creating framework for pupils' self-discipline | | |
| Getting attention | | |
| Manner and use of teacher praise and positive reinforcement | | |
| Clear lesson structure: do the pupils know what is expected to happen? | | |
| Room arranged appropriately for lesson | | |
| Resources readily available and appropriate | | |
| Dismissing the class | | |

*Figure 9.6* Lesson observation: this form has a focus on classroom management – an issue for many inexperienced teachers. It allows the observer to comment on strengths and points to watch

| | Name | | Date | |
|---|---|---|---|---|
| | Class being observed | | Observer | |
| Behavioural issue | | Intervention & Impact | | Alternative? |
| 1. | | | | |
| 2. | | | | |
| 3. | | | | |
| 4. | | | | |
| 5. | | | | |
| 6. | | | | |
| 7. | | | | |
| 8. | | | | |
| 9. | | | | |

Figure 9.7 Lesson observation: this form has a focus on managing behaviour and looking at teacher interventions. It allows the observer to comment on the impact of the teacher's intervention on specific behaviours and suggest alternatives

| Teacher: | Subject/Year/Group: | |
|---|---|---|
| Observer: | Attendance: Boys | Girls |
| | Total | |

| Focus of lesson observation: | | |
|---|---|---|

| Prompts | Comments | Date/Period/Time: |
|---|---|---|
| Punctual start | **Context summary:** classroom displays and management, lesson content, methods & strategies, activities, organisation, role of any support staff/adults in the room and external disruptions | |
| Preparation and planning | | |
| Register taken | | |
| Clear context, aims/objectives, instructions & explanations | | |
| Praise good behaviour and work | | |
| Redirects off-task behaviour calmly | | |
| Consequences given calmly | **Strengths of the lesson:** | |
| Positive re-enforcement | | |
| Feedback to students | | |
| High expectations & purposeful atmosphere | | |
| Students understand what they are doing, how well they have done and how they can improve | **Areas for further development:** | |
| Students actively participate in the lesson | | |
| Homework | | |
| Plenary | | |
| Teacher's comments: | | Signatures & Date Teacher Observer |

*Figure 9.8* Lesson observation: this form is a format for a general observation that the observer would write on during the lesson and pick out strengths and areas for further development. Perhaps it tries to do too much

**Supplementary Notes for Classroom Observations**

*Guidance on routine procedures*
* Students and teachers must follow policies and procedures.
1 Students and teachers should arrive punctually.
2 Students should enter the teaching room in an orderly way, as organised by the teacher.
3 Students should sit as directed by the teacher.
4 Students should prepare immediately for the lesson by:
   i removing outerwear, and storing as directed;
   ii removing bags and taking out necessary equipment (diary, pen, pencil, ruler, rubber, organiser).
5 The teacher should set clear aims/objectives for the lesson.
6 The teachers and students should review and evaluate the lesson in light of the objectives set.
7 Students should leave the teaching room in an orderly way, and promptly on the pips, so that they can arrive at their next lesson on time.

*Consider:*
Preparation and planning – linked to whole college policies and schemes of work.
Context of lesson set – past, present and future, cross curricular.
Classroom management – use of policies.
Positive re-enforcement – use of positive repetition, tangible rewards, catch students being good.
Feedback to students – linked to whole college policies, verbal and written.
Students actively participate in the lesson are productive, work at good pace, show interest, sustain concentration and understand tasks.
Homework – in line with policy, to consolidate, extend coverage of work, aims of homework explained.
Plenary – review what students have learnt at the end of the lesson, looking ahead.

*Teachers' effectiveness is indicated by:*
• clarity of exposition,
• use and timing of questions,
• high levels of time on task,
• review at the end of the lesson,
• sharing of lesson's objectives with students,
• humour?
• maintain variety and pace of activities,

continued

*Box 9.2* A secondary school's supplementary list of features of effective teaching for staff to use when observing any teacher

- hold and communicate high academic and behavioural expectations,
- establish and follow whole college and subject teaching classroom rules and procedures clearly,
- specify consequences and their relation to student behaviour,
- enforce rules promptly, consistently and equitably,
- share responsibility for classroom management with students,
- monitor activities and behaviour to provide feedback and reinforcement,
- spot, intervene and prevent misbehaviour quickly.

*Methods and strategies:*
Does the teacher:
- involve all students in the lesson?
- use a variety of activities/learning methods (including starter activity)?
- apply teaching methods appropriate to the NC?
- use a variety of questioning techniques to probe for knowledge and understanding, and to draw on student experiences and or ideas relevant to the lesson?
- encourage students to use a variety of problem-solving techniques?
- give clear instructions and explanations?
- listen and respond to students?
- ensure that activities have a clear purpose in improving students' understanding or achievement?

*Assessment*
Does the teacher:
- focus on understanding and meaning? Factual memory? Skills mastery? Applications in real life settings?
- use tests and competitions to assess understanding?
- recognise misconceptions and clear them up?
- encourage students to do better next time?
- use the marking and presentation policy?

*Time resource management*
Does the teacher:
- structure the lesson to use the time available well?
- ensure lesson lasts for the planned time?
- use an appropriate pace?
- allocate their time fairly among students?

*Creating 'high expectations' depends upon:*
- degree of difficulty of work set and material used (degree of challenge),
- clear communication of standard and quality expected,
- view of what good work should look like shared with students along with learning objectives, assessment criteria and success criteria,
- insufficiently good work or responses challenged – orally or through marking,

- insistence on personal best standards and good presentation;
- encouraging depth and range of response,
- effective and high order questioning,
- ethos and climate – expectation of high standards with positive encouragement, confidence and ambition,
- provision of strong role model,
- praising and valuing of good work and responses,
- insistence on good order behaviour and application to and completion of work,
- allow students to take responsibility for their own learning,
- good pace of lesson.

*A lesson is likely to be unsatisfactory if any of the following are (significantly) present:*
- the teacher's knowledge of the subject is not good enough to promote demanding work,
- basic skills are not taught effectively,
- a significant minority of students are not engaged in lessons,
- lessons are poorly planned and organised leading to insufficient time on task,
- there are weaknesses in controlling the class,
- students do not know what they are doing.

## The post-observation discussion

Take some time to reflect. Think about the teaching and learning you have seen, focusing on strengths and a few areas for development. Be clear about your main message – this will take some thinking about. There is no point listing every little thing that went wrong. You need to have 'the big picture' in your mind in order to convey it to the teacher. Remember it needs to be useful to them – aim to help them develop. You want to avoid the extremes of crushing them or giving the impression that things are better than they really are. It is a very fine line to tread, but your knowledge of the context and the teacher will help you.

Attend to the physical setting of the discussion. Choose a place where you won't be disturbed – you never know how someone is going to react in a feedback. Position chairs at right angles to each other for the most conducive atmosphere. This enables you to have eye contact but not in the formal direct way that sitting opposite someone across a desk would ensure. However, there will be times when such a setting will help you get a tough message across. A cup of coffee and biscuits can be a useful ice-breaker and show that you value someone.

Be aware of your body language and notice the teacher's. A large proportion of communication is non-verbal, so:

- lean slightly forward,
- uncross arms,
- try to ignore any of your distracting inner thoughts,
- make eye-contact,
- smile and nod, and
- listen actively.

Try to ask questions to guide their thinking, but not in a way that intimidates or implies criticism. Encourage reflection and listen well by asking open-ended questions, such as:

- how do you think the lesson went?
- what were you most pleased with? Why?
- what were you trying to achieve?
- what did the pupils learn?
- what did the lower attaining pupils learn?
- what did the higher attaining pupils learn?
- why do you think the lesson went the way it did?
- why did you choose that activity?
- were there any surprises?
- when you did ... the pupils reacted by ... Why do you think that happened?
- could you help me understand what you took into account when you were planning?
- if you taught that lesson again, what, if anything, would you do differently?
- what will you do in the follow-up lesson?

Be aware of what you say, and how you say it. Focus on the teaching and learning that took place, using specific examples of what children said and did. Be fulsome and generous in identifying strengths and progress, but be clear about what needs to be developed. Avoid talking about yourself or other teachers you have seen unless this will be useful to the teacher. Comments such as, 'I would have ...' can be inappropriate and irritate and alienate the teacher. Aim for the teacher to do most of the talking and thinking.

Paraphrase and summarise what the teacher says. This helps you concentrate on what is being said and is very helpful in getting a clear shared understanding of what the teacher thinks. It involves reflecting back your interpretation of what you have heard, which can be very useful for the teacher. Use phrases such as, 'So what you mean is ...', 'In other words ...'. Be positive and up-beat throughout. Be sensitive to how the teacher is taking your feedback, and ease off if necessary – Rome was not built in a day.

*Box 9.3* The post-observation discussion (Bubb and Hoare 2001: 67–68)

# Chapter 10

# Assessment against the induction standards

Assessment against the standards is an essential facet of the induction process since it leads to the key judgement about whether NQTs will pass and continue their career or fail. This chapter examines what people think of the standards and addresses the assessment meetings and reports. It will consider what is meant to happen, what our research found was happening and outlines some good practice.

## The Induction Standards

The induction circular sets in place the requirements for the induction year. These are two-fold:

- by the end of the induction period NQTs should have continued to meet the Standards for the award of Qualified Teacher Status consistently,
- they should also have met all the induction standards.

Induction tutors liked having standards as fixed and universal criteria around which to judge teaching. There had never before been standards of any sort to assess NQTs against. The standards are, however, controversial.

### No allowance for context

Bleach is concerned that the standards do not allow for differences in school contexts (Bleach 1999: 20). NQTs in our research felt the iniquity of there being no allowance for the circumstances in which the standards are met. Some had deliberately chosen 'easy' schools for their first teaching post, because they worried about the effect a school with discipline problems would have on their induction year.

## Open to interpretation

The standards are open to interpretation. We found people who inter-preted them literally and others who had a very casual approach to what they meant – implying that they knew what a good teacher was and that was what counted. There was confusion as to what each standard actually meant. A very experienced induction tutor said:

> I think there is lots wrong with the standards. Standard A, I mean I can't honestly say I have ever really understood. I think it means plan lessons but [others don't] ... It's written in such a way that it could mean yearly targets, scheme of work for this unit, this lesson, or the next five minutes.

He spoke of an LEA induction tutor training course activity:

> We take the standards and we get the group to work out what the standards mean in plain English. Why is it necessary for teachers to interpret standards in order to be able to work on them?

## High expectations

Bleach believes that the expectation that NQTs should meet all the stand-ards is 'an over-estimation of what is possible'. Bubb too thinks that they are very demanding – 'they describe the best sort of teacher rather than a beginner' (Bubb 2001a: 38). Colin Richards, in a letter to the *Times Educational Supplement*, wrote:

> The [QTS] Standards represent an impossible set of demands which properly exemplified would need the omnicompetence of Leonardo da Vinci, the diplomatic expertise of Kofi Annan, the histrionic skills of Julie Walters, the grim determination of Alex Ferguson, and the saintliness of Mother Teresa, coupled with the omniscience of God.
>
> (Richards 2000)

Bleach feels that the standards should not be seen as things to pass or fail but which involve 'gradations in performance' (Bleach 2000a: 20).

Some standards expect cutting edge practice, such as target setting, that may not be developed in certain schools, and raise the question of how an NQT can be failed for not doing what the teacher in the room next door does not do. Some appear straightforward but actually contain huge com-plexities. For instance, induction standard (e) *takes account of ethnic and cultural diversity to enrich the curriculum and raise achievement*. This complex issue is written as if no problem existed – that achievement would automatically be raised if teachers take ethnic and cultural diversity into account when enriching the curriculum.

The Standards Framework, which was published in September 2001 (DfES 2001e), should make the Induction Standards clearer by setting them in the context not only of those for QTS but also those for threshold, subject leaders, SENCOs, advanced skills teachers and head teachers. Even so, it is clear that the induction standards build in very high expectations of new teachers.

### Repeat the QTS standards

Many NQTs considered that the induction standards repeated those for QTS and that this had repercussions for how they felt as professionals. They felt that they were not trusted, and nor was their qualified teacher status. It is the expectation of the NQT as being a fully qualified and trusted professional that appears to be seriously at odds with the perceived underlying motivation behind the policy – to catch people out, to test them again. It could be argued that the induction standards are the most significant 'carrier' of this perceived attitude. This NQT's views were common:

> The induction standards were like redoing the PGCE with several PGCE standards in one induction standard. The very idea of having to redo what you'd spent so much energy on in PGCE was depressing.

Many felt resentful that they had to go through another hurdle of assessment. Those who had done three- or four-year undergraduate teaching courses felt this most strongly.

Tickle is critical of the 'bureaucratic minimalism' of the induction regulations and is critical of the induction standards. He feels they are 'an insufficient selection of teaching elements' and 'nothing more than a minor supplement' to those for QTS (Tickle 2000a: 9). Alistair Tickett, writing at the end of his induction year, says the induction standards seem too much like those set in initial teacher training and that there should be more sense of progress built in. He suggests that standards should be linked to specific subjects (Tickett 2001: 15).

Tickle considers that personal qualities and professional characteristics such as respect for learners, patience, interpersonal sensitivity and reliability should be included in the induction standards. Though laudable, such qualities would be very hard to assess. Tickle also thinks that there should be a place for local or individualised specifications negotiated between induction tutor and the NQT, and is keen for NQTs to carry out practitioner research (Tickle 2000b: 711).

### Interpreting the standards

As we have said, induction tutors liked having standards as fixed and universal criteria around which to judge teaching. However, they were unsure of how to interpret the standards, saying, 'It's a sharp but very blunt tool too' and that they encouraged general rather than specific comments. Some felt a need for something more concrete:

> You have all the nebulous stuff about policies and working with IEPs and all this, but actually what do you do when a kid calls you a dickhead, and then says that's not swearing?

### Familiarity with the standards

The induction circular states that NQTs should be familiar with the induction standards and they should monitor their own work in relation to them. However, 11 per cent of NQTs in our research said they were not familiar with the Induction Standards at the start of their induction period. This represents a large number of new teachers.

Teacher training institutions need to ensure that the induction standards are explained, and the TTA has produced materials to help this process (TTA 2001c). In order to raise the profile of the induction period, one ITE provider runs a conference week at the end of their course which bridges initial training and induction. This allows trainees to engage with the induction period in a clear, explicit manner and as part of the CPD process. Time is given to explain the whole process, engage with the induction standards in relation to those for QTS, and to complete the Career Entry Profiles.

It is also important that induction tutors refer to the induction standards as soon as NQTs start at their school, so that everyone is clear about how the assessment of induction works. We found that NQTs and induction tutors valued courses that explained the induction standards and the whole assessment process.

### The assessment of the standards by head teachers

Another issue is that assessment against the standards is in the hands of school staff who may have little experience of judging what is 'good enough'. Evidence gained in OFSTED inspections does not form part of the induction assessment, although in the consultation exercise on the statutory regulations this was suggested (DfEE 1998a). OFSTED has a role in quality assurance of induction in its regular inspection of schools and LEAs: a judgement is made on the arrangements for induction (OFSTED 1999; OFSTED 2001b). However, it is the head teacher and induction tutor who make the key recommendation about whether an NQT is meeting the standards. This is potentially problematic, as one induction tutor in our research pointed out:

> You could get some zealot in some school, some Head of Department who is a personality, who gets a pretty good NQT and ends up failing them, and also is the type of dogmatic person who sticks to their guns. Some good NQTs could end up failing or only passed after a lot of hoo ha.

OFSTED found that, in both primary and secondary schools, NQTs were observed by teachers who were not fully familiar with the QTS and induction standards. In most schools, all staff involved in induction needed further training in assessing NQTs against the induction standards (OFSTED 2001c: para. 39).

### How to demonstrate the standards

The phrasing of both the standards for QTS and those for induction require those being assessed to 'demonstrate' them. This caused confusion and a variety of practice. Some NQTs felt the standards lacked clarity and were inflexible in their wording. Many were unsure of what they had to do to demonstrate that they were meeting the standards:

> To be honest I haven't got a clear understanding of what the process is. They gave us this huge folder but it wasn't really explained what we needed to do, whether we had to keep any evidence of things ourselves.

This resulted in some NQTs being expected to keep teaching practice level files of evidence:

> I think it's absolutely obscene the amount of paperwork and the amount of standards that you're having to meet and the evidencing is absolutely over the top, way beyond what we should have to do.

This happened in a school which was part of an SCITT, where NQTs appear to have been treated like students rather than qualified teachers. They had to keep many large portfolios of evidence against each of the standards. This included, for instance, logging all contact with parents as evidence for induction standard (g). Others did no extra paperwork for induction. The disparity between the two caused confusion and resentment, particularly when NQTs from different schools met at courses.

Some three-quarters of NQTs said that they evaluated their work in relation to the induction standards. Again, one wonders what the others did – and why. It appears that they followed their own and the school's lead in what they should be doing. For instance, an NQT in a reception class set objectives for and spent a great deal of time getting certificates to be a qualified swimming teacher and for first aid. Though useful, these were neither related to the induction standards nor to classroom practice. They were, however, useful to the school and the NQT. Here there is a tension about what induction aims to do and whom it aims to benefit.

### Were the induction standards useful?

By and large, induction tutors and head teachers found the induction standards useful, but NQTs did not:

> I feel that the induction process and CEP were a headache – extra bits of paper to fill in when you don't have time – I don't feel it's necessary! I trained for three years, isn't that enough?

There was a feeling that the first year of teaching is stressful enough and that induction, rather than easing this, made it worse through school demands and the threat of failure.

> The induction standards and proving you've reached them added stress in a very full, hectic and busy year and thus they're not that helpful ... there should be less form-filling ... and proving that we've done mundane tasks.

Some NQTs took the demonstration of the standards so seriously they put at risk their own well-being. One NQT whose teaching everyone rated extremely highly, spent hours every week filing evidence of how she was meeting the standards and was disappointed when she realised that there would be no formal assessment occasion where she could show anyone the fruits of her labour. The DfES or TTA should state exactly what level of evidence is required. In most cases, we consider that no extra work needs to be gathered by the NQT since all the standards should be met through the everyday teaching in a school for a year.

Many NQTs complained about the assessment process being bureaucratic, but an induction tutor pointed out that it depended on the quality of the NQT:

> Where you've got a NQT who's on track and is doing well then the bureaucracy is little more than just a tick box exercise which has an inbuilt element of reflection.

However, it was more useful for weak NQTs:

> If it's sensitively handled, you can use that process to help them develop, and certainly in the cases of some NQTs it might be the way that they decide that it's not the right career choice.

## Assessment meetings and reports

### What is meant to happen

The induction circular states that there should be formal assessment meetings and reports at the end of each of the three terms. The meetings should be held towards the end of each term, and are the forum for the termly assessment reports to be discussed and written. They should be seen as significantly different from the other meetings between the NQT and induction tutor because they are a summary of progress so far. Another difference is that the head teacher should attend this meeting. Standardised forms have to be filled in and sent to the Appropriate Body within ten days of the meeting. Each Appropriate Body sets its own deadlines for reports.

### What does happen

OFSTED found that, though schools' assessments were almost always accurate enough for the purpose, a small minority made them with no specific reference to the standards. McLeod reported that knowledge of the QTS standards was essential but lacking in many induction tutors (McLeod 2000: 45). Bubb found that they wanted to have clear examples of what an average NQT's achievement of them would look like and, currently, their interpretation of what was good enough varied and this is felt to be unfair by NQTs. Moreover, different levels of understanding of what the standards meant were also demonstrated in the termly assessment forms and the objectives. Induction tutors who also supervised students on teaching practice had a better understanding than those who were unfamiliar with a standards-based model of training (Bubb 2000b: 6).

In our research, 81 per cent of respondents had an assessment meeting at the end of each term. Slightly more – 86 per cent – had an assessment report at the end of each term. Such results suggest that some NQTs (5 per cent) must have received an assessment report without having had an end of term assessment meeting.

### Organising the meeting

Teachers should have their own individual report and assessment meeting. Because of its more formal nature, it is worth thinking about assessment meetings carefully. The venue needs to be chosen carefully. The TTA recommends:

> The best setting is likely to be one that is conducive to a private professional discussion, where all involved will feel comfortable and where there is very little likelihood of being interrupted or overheard.
>
> (TTA 1999d: 11)

Holding the meeting in the NQT's classroom gives them a feeling of control that may not be present in the head teacher's office. It also means that there is easy access to further evidence, such as children's work. Head teachers should attend the meeting, especially since they will have to sign the assessment form. In many secondary schools, however, this did not happen. Induction managers were delegated this responsibility entirely. In schools where the head teacher attended the meeting, they found it a good opportunity to gain and contribute detailed information about the new teacher's progress. Occasionally, however, the presence of the head teacher unnerved and inhibited the NQTs.

In most schools, a date was chosen well in advance that was convenient to all. The length of the meetings varied depending on the degree of agreement about the NQT's performance and how much preparatory work on the report had been done. Most took about half an hour. Some schools wrote an agenda such as the one in Figure 10.1 so that everyone understood the focus of different parts of the meeting. The agenda also formalised the meeting.

---

INDUCTION PERIOD – TERM 1
Assessment meeting between NQT, induction tutor and head teacher
10th December 4.00 – 4.30pm.
Venue: NQT's classroom

AGENDA

1 Clarification of purpose of meeting: to read and amend the draft assessment report form.
2 Assessment of Planning, Teaching and Class Management.
3 Assessment of Monitoring, Assessment, Recording, Reporting and Accountability.
4 Assessment of Other Professional Requirements.
5 NQT to make written comment during or after the meeting.

---

*Figure 10.1* Sample agenda for the first assessment meeting (adapted from TTA 1999d: 12)

### Evidence to inform the assessment meeting

The assessment meeting should be based on evidence. This may take various forms, such as:

- records of observations – there should be at least two a term,
- records from meetings with the induction tutor and other staff,
- self-assessment by the NQT,
- any monitoring of the NQT's planning, assessment and pupils' work,
- any information about the NQT's work with others such as the SENCO, parents and colleagues.

Schools did not find it necessary to collect large amounts of supporting evidence, but selected specific pieces of evidence that arose from the NQT's day-to-day work, and from the induction monitoring and support programme.

### Writing the report

There are two versions of the assessment form – the original (see Figure 10.2), and one that can be used to build up a cumulative record. The first page of the form consists of information about the NQT and school, and some tick boxes; the second requires writing under the three induction standard headings; and the third is for the NQT to comment, and for the head teacher, induction tutor and NQT to sign.

The form for the first and second terms requires the head teacher to tick one of two statements:

> The above named teacher's progress indicates that he/she will be able to meet the requirements for the satisfactory completion of the induction period.

> The above named teacher is not making satisfactory progress towards the requirements for the satisfactory completion of the induction period.
>
> (DfEE 2000a: Annex B)

Deciding which box to tick was straightforward in the majority of cases we encountered. However, many people said that they would like some intermediate statement because they were concerned about their NQT's performance but wouldn't go so far as to say that it was unsatisfactory. It can be difficult to balance professional honesty with the need to keep the NQT motivated enough to try to improve. However, the Appropriate Body needs to be alerted to any weak NQTs so that they can take appro-

## NQT Induction assessment form for the:

☐ End of first assessment period.　　　　　　　☐ End of second assessment period.

- This form should be completed by the Headteacher and sent to the Appropriate Body within ten working days of the relevant assessment meeting.
- Where tick boxes appear, please insert 'X' to the relevant box(es).

Full name

Date of birth

DfES reference number of NQT　　　　　　　　　　　/

National insurance number of NQT

Name of school

DfES number of school

**Second period assessment:**
Is this the school that reported at the end of the first period?　　☐ Yes　　☐ No

Name of appropriate body receiving the report

Date of appointment

NQT's Specialism　　　　☐ Key stage　▶ Please specify

☐ Age range　▶ Please specify

☐ Subject　▶ Please specify

Does the NQT work:　　☐ Part-time?　▶ Please specify proportion of a week worked

☐ Full-time?

**Recommendation:**　☐ **The above named teacher's progress indicates that he/she will be able to meet the requirements for the satisfactory completion of the induction period.**

☐ **The above named teacher is not making satisfactory progress towards the requirements for the satisfactory completion of the induction period.**

Please indicate the kinds of support and monitoring arrangements that have been in place this term.

☐ Observations of the NQT's teaching and provision of feedback.

☐ Discussions between the NQT and the induction tutor to review progress and set targets.

☐ Observations of experienced teachers by the NQT.

☐ An assessment meeting between the NQT and the induction tutor.

☐ Other　▶ Please specify

Induct1(Word2000)　　　　　　　　　　　　　　　　　　　1

*Continued*

*Figure 10.2* Assessment form (DfES 2000a: Annex B)

- Under the following headings, please give brief details of:
  - the extent to which the NQT is meeting the induction standards.
  - in circumstances where the NQT **is not** considered to have made satisfactory progress, details of the following should also be given in the relevant sections:
    - areas of weakness;
    - evidence used to inform the judgement;
    - targets for the coming term; and
    - the support which is planned.

  Reference should be made to the specific standards concerned.
- Please continue on a separate sheet if required.

Planning, teaching and class management.

Monitoring, assessment, recording, reporting and accountability.

Other professional requirements.

**Comments by the NQT:** I have discussed this report with the induction tutor and/or headteacher and:

☐ have no comments to make. ☐ wish to make the following comments.
▼

School stamp/validation

**Signed:**

| | | | |
|---|---|---|---|
| **Headteacher**<br>(if different from<br>Induction tutor) | | Date | |
| **Full name**<br>(CAPITALS) | | | |
| **NQT** | | Date | |
| **Full name**<br>(CAPITALS) | | | |
| **Induction tutor** | | Date | |
| **Full name**<br>(CAPITALS) | | | |

priate action. Most appeals have been granted where NQTs' first term's forms had the 'satisfactory' box ticked. NQTs can then say that they had insufficient warning that the school considered their progress towards meeting the induction standards inadequate.

The school must also tick the kinds of monitoring and support that have been in place during the term. These are:

- observations of the NQT's teaching and provision of feedback,
- discussions between the NQT and the induction tutor to review progress and set objectives,
- observations of experienced teachers by the NQT,
- an assessment meeting between the NQT and the induction tutor.

(DfEE 2000a: Annex B)

All should be ticked if the school is complying with the induction regulations, and any omissions will alert the Appropriate Body that things are not happening as they should.

## Writing about the induction standards

The bulk of the report involves writing briefly under three headings about the extent to which the NQT is meeting the standards. In areas where the NQT is not considered to have made satisfactory progress, weaknesses should be clearly outlined with evidence, objectives for the following term should be set and the support planned.

We found that strong reports had the following features. They:

- focused on areas covered by the standards,
- contained a good level of detail,
- were selective about significant strengths and weaknesses,
- had a clear message in the first sentence,
- appeared to have chosen words carefully,
- were well written and concise.

Where reports were weak they:

- had little detail,
- were not clear about how well the standards are being met,
- were not completed at the end of term, but during the following term,
- did not write about areas mentioned in the standards,
- omitted key topics such as behaviour management and planning,
- were nearly identical to others from the same school,
- had comments in the wrong boxes,
- were undeservedly glowing,

- were contradictory, e.g. the text said the NQT was doing very well, but the targets indicated weaknesses in behaviour management and planning,
- made too little use of the box indicating that the NQT was not making progress,
- had spelling and grammatical errors.

### Good practice in completing the induction assessment form

Induction tutors reported that they took about two hours to write each report. The case study below shows how one induction tutor went about writing the report.

---

**Case study: how Jo completed the assessment on William**

Both Jo and the NQT evaluated how they thought William was meeting the standards by jotting notes on the format in Figure 10.3. They discussed their views, ensuring that evidence existed for all assertions. She drafted sections of the report against the three headings of the standards aiming for a word length of 300 words. She wrote an overall message in the first sentence and then elaborated. Where space allowed, she referred briefly to evidence.

Jo gave a copy to the head teacher and William to look at just before the meeting. At the meeting all discussed what was written and suggested changes.

The revised agreed document was then given to William for a written comment, and then he, Jo and the head teacher signed it. All were given copies and the original was sent to the Appropriate Body.

---

Boxes 10.1 and 10.2 are examples of completed sections of reports. Their styles are useful to analyse. Box 10.1 is brief, impersonal and entirely focused on the induction standards. It makes no reference to those for QTS or to evidence for the judgements. Box 10.2 contains a selection of more detailed prose-based paragraphs written about different NQTs.

## What people in our research thought of their reports

Overall, NQTs were happy with their reports: 48 per cent described the assessment reports as 'very accurate' and 38 per cent as 'quite accurate'. This can be celebrated as demonstrating a high level of skill by schools.

| Date:                              NQT: | Induction tutor: |
|---|---|
| Planning, teaching and class management – strengths | Planning, teaching and class management – areas for development |
| Monitoring, assessment, recording, reporting and accountability – strengths | Monitoring, assessment, recording, reporting and accountability – areas for development |
| Other professional requirements – strengths | Other professional requirements – areas for development |

*Figure 10.3* Summary notes for the end of term assessment – to be used by the induction tutor and NQT (Bubb 2000c: 98)

**Planning, teaching and class management**

a NQT sets clear targets for his pupils and employs a variety of teaching strategies. He monitors pupils' progress carefully.

b Planning is effective and takes account of pupils' differences. More needs to be done on self-evaluation to inform lesson planning.

c Pupils' behaviour in lessons is of a high order with appropriate rules being set and high expectations.

d Planning to meet the needs of pupils with Special Educational Needs is taking place though some work needs to be done on high achievers.

e Is clearly taking account of ethnic and cultural diversity.

**Monitoring, assessment, recording, reporting and accountability**

f Pupils' work is regularly and thoroughly assessed according to the Department's policy. Needs to develop ability to assess against outside benchmarks and to inform students of their achievement and to use assessment to inform planning more rigorously.

g Regular assesssment sheets are filled in on time with informative feedback provided. However, more regular feedback could be provided as and when appropriate.

**Other professional requirements**

h Not really appropriate for PE as there is no support available in class.

i As and when apropriate, takes responsibility for implementation of school policies and for pupils' behaviour generally. Has successfully dealt with a case of low-level bullying in one of his classes, employing school policies.

j Is taking responsibility for own development, has attended INSET on trampolining, dance and more general INSET at the Institute of Education and the LEA NQT meetings. Needs to continue to develop understanding and knowledge of GCSE and AS/A2 courses.

*Box 10.1* A completed report – secondary PE

Nevertheless, the 7 per cent who felt that the assessment reports were not accurate is a cause for concern. Since there is meant to be a regular dialogue throughout the year, there should be no surprises.

In our research we found several cases of poor practice, such as NQTs whose first term assessment meeting and report did not take place until the end of the second term. One said, 'I have never seen the written reports.' This is disturbing as the reports should be signed by the NQT.

One wonders what happened to the 14 per cent of NQTs who did not have an assessment report at the end of each term. How did the Appropriate Body know how they were doing? Did the NQTs pass their induction period satisfactorily or did the outstanding paperwork mean that they did

## Planning, teaching and class management

*Example: Keith (Bubb 2000c: 100)*
Keith is making good progress. He plans effectively and has followed the policy of the school. He works in partnership with the other year group teacher. He identifies appropriate teaching objectives and specifies clearly how they will be taught. He sets relevant, demanding tasks for the children and has been observed using effective teaching strategies for whole class, groups and individuals. His planning is also clearly differentiated to meet the needs of the pupils. The standard of behaviour of the pupils is high, with appropriate rules and expectations well established. The school's behaviour policy is followed. The classroom itself is tidy, well organised and is a stimulating learning environment which communicates enthusiasm for what is being taught.

There are a number of children in the class on the SEN register, including one with a statement. Current IEPs are in place and, in consultation with the SENCO, clear objectives have been set, and these are referred to when planning. There is also regular collection of evidence to monitor progress.

*Example: Tony (TTA 1999d: 28)*
Tony is making satisfactory progress in some areas, but not in others.

Observations of Tony's teaching show that he has built excellent relationships with his pupils. Their behaviour is generally good and Tony handles inappropriate behaviour well.

Tony makes good use of the school's long- and medium-term planning frameworks, but pupils' work suggests that his short-term planning for specific classes continues to be insufficiently focused on improving his pupils' achievement. There is little differentiation and Tony tends to focus his teaching on the more able pupils, accepting underachievement too readily. He needs to make considerable progress in this aspect of his teaching in order to meet the induction requirements.

In the second term, Tony has agreed to renew the objective of developing his ability to set appropriate learning objectives for *all* of his pupils and using these as a basis for his planning and teaching. He will aim to develop his mathematics teaching further, but has also agreed a new objective relating to raising his expectations of pupil achievement in literacy. Tony has found it particularly useful to observe the practice of other teachers in this and another school, and this will be a key element of his support this term. Further support will also be provided by Tony's induction tutor and by the school's literacy and mathematics coordinators.

## Monitoring, assessment, recording, reporting and accountability

*Example: Paul (Bubb 2000c: 101)*
Paul is making satisfactory progress in this area. He is now very reflective about his teaching and the strengths and weaknesses of individual pupils. He uses a variety of assessment methods including structured observations, testing and marking. He now completes his analysis of these systematically and uses the records to inform his planning. Paul is beginning to set specific

targets for individuals and groups in literacy and to use those to make purposeful interventions in learning. With the help of the parallel class teacher, he is also beginning to analyse results, looking for trends to check whether his pupils are making progress against attainment objectives. Paul has participated in one formal parents'/carers' meeting successfully and has made himself available to discuss appropriate objectives and give advice regarding support at home.

*Example: Riffat (Nursery) (Bubb 2000c: 101)*
Riffat's practice in this area is exemplary. Her assessments are of a very high quality and she monitors her observations to ensure children have been observed in all curriculum areas. Her records are extremely well kept and have been used as an example of good practice for staff and visitors. Riffat has tackled writing reports for the first time and was able successfully to summarise observations from other staff to give accurate portraits of her key children. Because Riffat's records and assessments were so good she was able to report accurately and effectively at parents' evening.

**Other professional requirements**

*Example: Theresa (Bubb 2000c: 102)*
Theresa is responsible for one support staff member and a number of parents/carers who have volunteered to work in the room. She is trialling a new school initiative to formalise communications with these people and is recording learning intentions and objectives for the children that the additional adult works with. Theresa has read the school's policies and has implemented many of them well. She seeks support to address incidences of bullying to show both children and parents/carers how seriously she takes them.

Theresa willingly participates in school-based INSET. She writes reflective notes after attending induction sessions at the professional development centre.

*Example: Ann (based on TTA 1999d: 26)*
Ann has failed to meet the standards in this area. She has made consistent efforts to take school-wide policies on board, but has been unable to implement them effectively because of her difficulties with classroom management. She has taken care to involve learning support teachers in the planning of lessons they support, but during the teaching of lessons has found it difficult to work collaboratively and often expects the support teacher to take full responsibility for addressing the needs of pupils who are experiencing difficulty.

Ann has experienced difficulties in playing a constructive role in her own professional development. Although responding positively to the support provided, she has not found it possible to implement the practical suggestions offered, with the result that many of her difficulties with her professional practice have persisted.

*Box 10.2 Examples of paragraphs from different NQTs' reports*

not? In Chapter 6 we discussed how difficult it was for Appropriate Bodies to get hold of assessment reports and how some had resorted to only releasing the £1,000 per term funding when reports had been received.

## Feedback on assessment forms

Induction tutors have complained that they get no feedback from their Appropriate Body, feeling that the reports gets sent off 'into the ether' without so much as an acknowledgement slip to say that they have arrived. One LEA gives written feedback on the first assessment report (see Box 10.3). This is a valuable quality assurance procedure and gives head

---

Copy to head teacher, induction tutor and LEA chief inspector

Dear Colleagues,

Thank you for the assessment form on X. Last year many induction tutors said that they would like feedback on the assessment reports that they wrote about their NQTs. I would like to make the following points about X's report.

- The report is a little thin bearing in mind that it should summarise progress against all the QTS and induction standards. There are many key areas, such as behaviour management and relating to parents, which are not commented upon.
- It would be useful to start each section in the report with a clear statement such as 'X is making insufficient / satisfactory / good / very good progress in all / most of / some of this area', and then give details. This would give the NQT and the LEA a clearer picture.
- I am a little confused by the signature dates. The head teacher has signed it on 12 December but the NQT and induction tutor did not sign it until 26 January and the LEA did not receive it until 14 February. Reports are meant to be written and discussed at the formal assessment meeting at the end of term. Please contact us to explain this contravention of the induction regulations.
- It is good to see that X made a comment on the report and that she feels well supported by her induction tutor.

I hope that this has been helpful. If you would like further guidance the next induction tutor training session for primary and secondary schools at the PDC is on 2 March 13.15–16.00.

Yours sincerely,

Induction Consultant

---

*Box 10.3* LEA feedback on a first-term assessment report

teachers and induction tutors a clear picture of how well they have completed the form, ideas for improvements and, most importantly, an opportunity for dialogue about NQTs' progress. The LEA has found that this investment of time has reaped rewards in terms of ensuring that all reports are written to a consistent high standard, and that schools feel reassured by the feedback.

## NQTs at risk of failing

The consequences of failing the induction period are huge. They will not be able to work in a maintained school or non-maintained special school again. One school that had an NQT who did not satisfactorily complete induction offered the advice in Box 10.4.

Where NQTs do not prove themselves to be successful teachers during their induction year, schools and Appropriate Bodies need to consider failing them. This only involves a very small number. In the first year of statutory induction only forty-five NQTs failed, and 16,000 passed. However, anyone failing induction is never allowed to teach in a maintained or non-maintained school again, ever. Induction cannot be repeated.

## The appeal procedure

It is important to understand the appeal procedure. This is written in Annex D of the induction circular. All those involved in appeals – the induction tutors, head teachers and LEA staff, as well as NQTs – reported that they were very stressful.

If an NQT fails induction, or has the induction period extended by the Appropriate Body, that body must tell the NQT of the right to appeal, who to appeal to, and the time limit for appeal (DfEE 2000a: Annex D).

The NQT must send a notice of appeal to the GTC (the Appeal Body) within 20 days of the date that the NQT received notice of the Appropriate Body's decision. This is problematic since it would generally take place during school holidays. The 'notice of appeal' letter should include all of the following information:

a    the NQT's name and address,
b    their DfES reference number and date of birth,
c    the name and address of the school which employed at the end of the induction period,
d    the name and address of their employer, if not the school,
e    the grounds of appeal,
f    the name, address and profession of anyone representing the NQT,
g    whether the NQT wants an oral hearing or not.

**Early intervention**
It is essential that early steps are taken to identify any difficulties an NQT is experiencing, to make sure that the support programme is revised and adapted to take account of these needs.

*Unambiguous, accurate records*
Induction tutors need to take a lot of care with the wording of observation summaries and review meeting records. Positive achievements need to be recognised, but at the same time, difficulties and weaknesses must be brought into the open.

*The induction standards should be the main focus*
The main focus should be on supporting the NQT to meet the induction standards – especially if the NQT is experiencing difficulties. All records should make this focus clear.

*The NQT must be fully aware of concerns and know how they will be supported*
Take time to explain to the NQT that everyone is working to support his or her progress. It is important for NQTs to understand their responsibility to act on the advice given and to take advantage of their support programme to move forward positively and successfully.

*Communicate concerns at an early stage to the Appropriate Body*
As soon as problems occur, talk to the LEA induction coordinator or link adviser/consultant to discuss the issues and organise appropriate external support from a specialist adviser.

*Encourage the NQT to raise any concerns s/he may have.*
All NQTs should know the school's and LEA's procedures for raising concerns about their induction.

*Keep careful records of meetings*
It is particularly important that records are made, that they are dated and signed, and that a note is kept of to whom they are given.

*Support for the induction tutor*
Because of the implications for the NQT's career, the induction tutor role becomes particularly demanding once it is clear that an NQT is experiencing difficulties. The induction tutor may need more support, such as:
- release time in addition to that initially allocated,
- regular and active support from senior management, including,
  - advice about next steps,
  - support in making judgements about the NQT's progress,
  - help with action plans and observation records, to make sure they are specific and well targeted,
  - support at review meetings.

*Box 10.4* Advice on NQTs at risk of failing the induction standards (based on TTA 2001b: 33–34)

The NQT must sign the appeal for it to be valid.

Grounds for appeal often focus on the NQT not being sufficiently supported and not getting their entitlement, particularly the 10 per cent reduced timetable. The other frequent ground for appeal is that the assessment reports did not make clear the extent of the problem. In some cases, for the first report the school decided to tick the statement:

> The above named teacher's progress indicates that he/she will be able to meet the requirements for the satisfactory completion of the induction period.

Thus the NQT was only told officially that their progress was unsatisfactory at the end of the second term, leaving them little time to improve before the final report.

The NQT has to send the following additional material with the appeal:

a   a copy of the document from the Appropriate Body notifying the NQT of its decision,
b   a copy of any document from the Appropriate Body outlining its reasons for coming to this decision,
c   a copy of every other document on which the NQT relies for the appeal.

NQTs can amend or withdraw their grounds of appeal or any part of their appeal material and they can also submit new material in support of the appeal up to the date they receive notice of the appeal hearing date (or notice of the outcome of the appeal if it is decided without a hearing).

The Appropriate Body has twenty working days from receiving the notice of appeal to reply. If the Appropriate Body decides at any time that it does not want to uphold the disputed decision, it should inform the Appeal Body, who will allow the appeal. The reply must contain:

a   the name and address of the Appropriate Body,
b   whether it seeks to uphold the disputed decision,
c   where it seeks to uphold the decision
   i   its answer to each of the NQT's grounds of appeal
   ii   whether it requests an oral hearing
   iii   the name, address, and profession of anyone representing the Appropriate Body.

The Appropriate Body should also send any document on which it wishes to rely to oppose the appeal, and, if the NQT has not supplied it, a copy of the written statement giving its reasons for the decision.

The next chapter concludes the book by considering the benefits of induction overall and its place in continuing professional development.

# Chapter 11

# Induction and continuing professional development

It is clear that induction is meant to be a bridge from initial teacher education and training to the profession, leading into continuing professional development and fitting into the processes and procedures of performance management in schools. This chapter will consider the extent to which this is successfully taking place and provide a framework for educators to work together to improve the potential of induction to dovetail with wider continuing professional development initiatives. The contours of best practice will be portrayed in such a way as to give all those involved in induction a point of reference from which to judge, in their own context, how new entrants can be given the best possible start to their professional lives and teaching career. In order to do this we shall be considering the points of view of head teachers, induction tutors and NQTs themselves as well as drawing on wider perspectives.

## Induction and teacher effectiveness

One of the main purposes behind the induction policy is to increase teacher effectiveness. This is hard to measure, but John Howson's analysis of OFSTED teaching grades shows that standards amongst NQTs continue to improve. Almost half of all lessons taught by NQTs seen during OFSTED inspections throughout the 1999/2000 school year were graded between 'excellent' and 'good' (Howson 2001: 24). How much of this improvement can be said to result from statutory induction provision, however, is hard to say.

There is overwhelming agreement among head teachers and induction tutors that statutory induction is helping NQTs to be more effective teachers. The views of state school head teachers are representative of the groups we asked. Nearly 40 per cent said it had improved NQT effectiveness 'a substantial extent' and 50 per cent said it had done so 'quite substantially'. Ten per cent said it had improved effectiveness 'a little' and only 1 per cent said 'not at all'. It appears that schools without a history of strong practice in this area considered the impact to be greatest. Independent schools were most likely to think that their induction provision had improved to a substantial extent, with statutory induction. Around a quarter of independent principals and induction tutors reported this. The majority of respondents said provision had altered substantially and that it was now 'formalised' and 'uniform':

> The tradition was sink or swim: now we help to train Olympic athletes.

Head teachers and induction tutors in all sectors thought that making induction statutory had helped 'because schools have got to do it'. However, many said that their schools already had good induction practices, so that the difference between cohorts was not noticeable. A head teacher who had successfully supported many NQTs in the past, however, considered that:

> This new structure makes it much more rational and there's a clear pattern to what's going on, clear expectations ... We feel we've got far greater control of the way things develop under the new structure.

NQTs also considered that induction support had helped their professional development and effectiveness as teachers, as Table 11.1 shows:

Head teachers and induction tutors appreciate what statutory induction has given NQTs and reported on the consequences of a lack of monitoring, support and assessment previous to its introduction. Many NQTs thought that the structure of induction had speeded their progress, enabling them to get to grips early on with aspects such as using assessment to inform planning. Some NQTs, however, commented that they did not consider that their induction entitlement had much part to play in their development, compared to other factors, such as experience, or 'the atmosphere of the school, the supportiveness of the staff'. One example is the NQT who said:

Table 11.1 NQTs' views of the contribution of statutory induction provision to their professional development

| | A great deal (%) | Quite a lot (%) | Not very much (%) | Not at all (%) |
|---|---|---|---|---|
| Contribution of induction support to professional development | 19 | 40 | 28 | 11 |
| How much progress has been made in teaching effectiveness during the year? | 59 | 34 | 4 | 1 |

Note
Percentage of NQT replies, aggregated from cohorts 1999–2000 and 2000–2001. There were minor differences between the two cohorts.

I do feel that my teaching developed hugely throughout my first year, but I don't think that this has any relation to the induction process. You learn as you teach and make mistakes.

Many head teachers and induction tutors thought that the structure of induction had accelerated the progress of their NQTs, enabling them to get to grips with aspects of teaching such as using assessment to inform planning, earlier than previously. Many thought that the policy had raised both the NQTs' and their own expectations of what should be achieved in the first year of teaching:

It has quite properly raised expectations that people will from a fairly early point be competent professionals who just lack experience, who don't lack competence.

The termly assessment meetings in particular were considered to have stopped people slackening off or 'stepping off the ladder' and kept them focused. One head teacher said that 'things aren't being accepted which will turn into bad habits and [create] bad teachers'.

Some NQTs thought that induction had helped them to be aware of the big picture, 'to consider all the different elements of teaching'. One NQT said it stopped her getting bogged down in the daily routine of teaching, concluding that 'left to yourself, you get blinkered'.

Statutory induction appears to be particularly beneficial when NQTs encounter problems, because schools are required to observe regularly, diagnose problems and support new teachers in remedying them. Our research found instances where it had prevented NQTs failing as teachers and failing their pupils. A primary head teacher talked about how the induction procedures had turned someone who was failing in the first term into not just a competent teacher, but also a very effective one:

Without this structured support ... the pupils would have been having a horrendous time, because there would be a teacher struggling and no guaranteed way of identifying that there was a problem.

In another case, the support, monitoring and assessment of the induction period convinced a very weak NQT that teaching was not for her.

There is some evidence that induction makes strong NQTs even more effective. One head teacher described an NQT as:

The kind of teacher who had she been left alone would still have done a darn good job. But because of the induction input we've had the opportunity to fine tune what she's doing.

## Continuing professional development

A commitment to lifelong learning and professional as well as personal development is at the heart of being part of a learning profession. If this commitment, with its associated activity, is to be regarded as a responsibility for all teachers, continuing professional development (CPD) will need to be presented as a continuum which extends from initial teacher education and training, through induction and early professional development and on into the whole of a teacher's career. The induction policy anticipates this and was introduced to provide a foundation for the long-term continuing professional development of new teachers.

The government launched its CPD strategy in 2001, stating that professional development is important for several reasons:

- the demands on teaching are changing all the time. Becoming and remaining a good teacher, keeping knowledge of curriculum subjects up to date, and being able to make the most of new technology all require continuing professional development.
- a strong professional development culture in a school frequently makes it a much better place to work, with open, supportive relationships, and more enthusiastic, self-confident staff.
- good professional development enables you to build the skills to enhance your career – whether that is in teaching, in education more widely, or beyond.
- schools which offer teachers regular opportunities for professional development find it easier to attract and retain good staff.
- we want pupils to develop enthusiasm for lifelong learning, since this is increasingly the key to success in adult life. That is more likely if they see their teachers involved in regular learning.

(DfES 2001c: 1)

CPD has increasingly come to replace the older concept of in-service training (INSET) as a way of configuring the ongoing development needs of teachers. In part this is because CPD, broadly defined, can more readily take account of both formal and informal learning opportunities and resonates with the increasing emphasis on lifelong education and learning which dominates our educational landscape.

CPD serves a range of purposes to meet the diverse needs of professionals in the field by providing the possibility of recurrent, incremental learning opportunities, accompanied by instruction, tutoring, coaching, mentoring or similar ongoing support. The aim of all CPD activities should be to bring about a change in the thinking and practice of participants, which in turn will have a positive impact in the workplace. Therefore, CPD should have the following impact:

- improving the thought and practice of teachers and their provision for students,
- developing the professional and personal knowledge, skills, experience, understanding and values of teachers,
- helping teachers to gain confidence and competence and maintain them,
- providing teachers with a means of valuing their learning and helping them demonstrate it to others,
- enabling teachers to see everyday practice situations as the actual source of professional learning.

### Induction in relation to continuing professional development

Our research suggests that the statutory induction arrangements are having a notable impact in areas of significant interest for educators who are concerned to capitalise on the potential benefits to the profession that may accrue from a more integrated approach to CPD. A number of factors have come to light that are worth pondering and may suggest ways of conceiving and implementing a more strategic approach to early professional development.

### Induction helps transition from training to the rest of a teacher's career

Three-quarters of state and independent school induction tutors felt that statutory induction had helped professional continuity and progression to a 'substantial' or 'quite substantial' extent. The views of induction tutors in sixth form colleges were similar. However, NQTs were less positive about statutory induction easing the transition between training and the rest of their career and professional development. One-third said that the school provision was limited in amount or poor in quality and that this explained their slow pace of progress. Comments such as 'I was left to it' and got assistance 'only when asked' were all too common.

Amongst the NQTs who were positive about induction building on their training some stated that, in contrast to when training, they were now employed doing the full job and all aspects of development were directly relevant to their working contexts. Others felt that they had time to reflect, could evaluate their work, develop specifically targeted areas and continued to learn. Some said that the quality of support was why progress had been made. In particular, support from staff across the school as well as induction tutors and observation feedback sessions were mentioned.

Many schools found that NQTs were used to setting themselves objectives from their training and that, in this, they had an advantage over others in the profession. Others felt that NQTs and induction tutors needed a great deal more guidance in setting objectives and drawing up action plans, in order for them to be most effective in aiding progress. Moreover, schools varied in the degree to which they helped NQTs to meet their objectives. Some left NQTs to meet them without giving any support. Others were very supportive:

> We have a commitment to help them reach those targets by providing appropriate development. Now that might be internally or it might be by sending people on appropriate courses.

This system of setting objectives was described by an induction tutor as 'proactive':

> Now we're saying make sure you make the most of your targets because it's going to drive your professional development.

Overall, head teachers and induction tutors feel that statutory induction is for the better in that it has formalised existing procedures. They use words such as 'formalise', 'rigour', 'thorough' and 'focused' when describing the consequences of adapting to or incorporating the induction requirements. Head teachers and induction tutors also felt that statutory induction had led to a heightening of awareness of the importance of meeting teachers' needs and implementing the policy in the minds of senior staff, especially Heads of Department. Accountability is also a common theme, typified by this comment:

> It is good that schools are now judged on how they support NQTs.

Implicit in responses from head teachers was that statutory induction is having some positive impact upon school staff in general and is reinforcing the ethos of professional development. One respondent said:

> We were close to achieving Investors In People status so our induction processes were well developed. It has helped crystallise the assessment side.

This is particularly interesting because of the links made between induction, staff development and the role induction has had in developing thinking about assessing performance of staff in general.

## Induction is a bridge to the rest of the career

Nearly two-thirds of induction tutors felt that induction had improved continuity and progression toward CPD to a 'substantial' or 'quite substantial' extent. The views of NQTs were even more positive than induction tutors. Three-quarters of NQTs felt that induction had provided a 'bridge' to assist their transition to Early Professional Development. Those who were negative felt that they had not been well supported during induction and that this disadvantaged them not only in relation to induction but also in relation to their longer-term career prospects.

Nevertheless, most NQTs felt their induction programme had prepared them to take responsibility for their own professional development in the future. Several NQTs and induction tutors commented upon the relation of induction to the second year of teaching. Many NQTs felt worried about how they would cope without the support that they had had during induction. Some thought that part of the induction period could be spent preparing for the second year, especially in training for curriculum coordination. Another told us:

> There is a very big difference in teaching in your second year – NQTs should be prepared for this as it has come as a shock – more responsibility of curriculum subject areas, more participation in school activities – assemblies, after school clubs, no reduced timetable or induction tutor, etc . . .

There was a wide range of needs identified for CPD. Many of these centred on subject leadership. However, needs at the end of the induction period were as individual as those set during induction because people were in different contexts and at different stages in their development. Several NQTs who we interviewed were given significant responsibilities in their second year – two became literacy coordinators in large comprehensives – and these additional responsibilities were not always adequately anticipated through targeted CPD.

## Induction fits into performance management

From September 2000 schools had to put in place a new performance management system that replaced appraisal. It includes:

- agreeing annual objectives for each teacher, including objectives relating to pupil progress and ways of developing and improving teachers' professional practice,
- in-year monitoring of progress and classroom observation of teachers,
- an end of year review meeting, which involves an assessment of teachers' overall performance, taking account of achievement against objectives, agreeing objectives for the coming year and discussion of professional development opportunities/activities.

(DfEE 2000b)

Threshold is linked to induction and performance management, as it is the next gatepost or opportunity for formal assessment. The threshold standards were considered similar to those for newly qualified teachers but built on and extended them through looking at pupil progress and wider professional effectiveness.

Everyone interviewed in the research was positive about how induction made a bridge between training and performance management. The similarities raised are summarised in Table 11.2.

*Table 11.2* Similarities and differences between induction and performance management

| Performance management structure | Induction similarities | Induction differences |
|---|---|---|
| Every teacher has a team leader | Every NQT has an induction tutor | |
| Annual objectives for each teacher | Objectives are set | Objectives set half termly |
| Objectives relate to pupil progress and ways of developing teachers' professional practice | Objectives relate to developing NQTs' professional practice | Objectives do not relate to pupil progress |
| Teachers develop professional practice | NQTs develop professional practice | NQTs have a 10 per cent reduced timetable for professional development activities |
| Monitoring of progress and classroom observation of teachers – at least one observation a year | NQTs monitored and observed | Half termly monitoring of progress including classroom observation – at least six a year |
| End of year review meeting involves an assessment of teachers' overall performance, taking account of achievement against objectives, agreeing objectives for the coming year and discussion of profession development opportunities/activities | NQTs also assessed | Review meetings every half term. Formal assessment meetings at end of each term |
| Using performance review outcomes to inform pay decisions | Outcomes relate to whether NQTs can stay in the profession | No link to pay |
| Statutory | Statutory as well | |

## Induction ties in with national incentives for CPD

The above analysis suggests that much has been achieved by NQTs, induction tutors, schools and Appropriate Bodies since the introduction of statutory induction in 1999. For the most part, NQTs are benefiting from the experiences and opportunities provided in schools/colleges. But generally both they and their induction tutors have indicated that while NQTs' professionalism is developing through their work, the importance of professional development occurring within a supportive whole-school framework cannot be stressed too much. Most schools/colleges have appreciated greatly the guidance and support provided by the DfES and the TTA and welcomed the framework of arrangements that have been put in place as part of the induction 'package'. But there is a need to go further and ensure that induction arrangements are located within the wider developmental matrix that is emerging as a key component of the new professionalism increasingly characterising teaching.

At the present time, the DfES and the General Teaching Council (GTC) are actively seeking to develop a consensus within the teaching profession of the parameters of CPD and thereby enhance teachers' expectations, both on entry to the profession and of their schools as professional learning communities. The government's strategy for teachers' continuing professional development, *Learning and Teaching* (DfES 2001c), incorporates a pilot programme of early professional development for teachers in their second and third years, building on the induction year. This is recognition of the fact that these are extremely important years for teachers in terms of retention and support at a key point in their careers. The aim is that teachers should have access to a wide range of developmental activities within a clearly focused framework of desired outcomes.

The GTC has already begun to influence the government's strategy for the professional development of teachers by focusing on securing a career-long entitlement to high-quality professional learning opportunities for all teachers that is properly resourced. Underpinning their work in the area of CPD is the development of a set of guiding expectations for teachers of the professional development experiences and outcomes which constitute 'entitlement'. These highlight areas such as self-review, engagement with research, updating professional and subject knowledge and networking with an expectation that the outcomes for teachers of professional learning and development will be both developing one's own practice and assisting in the development of the practice of colleagues (GTC 2001). Both are highly pertinent to induction.

Our own research on induction suggests that there is scope for schools/colleges to be intelligent at this juncture by reading the signals emanating from the government strategy and the GTC's professional development framework. They can then link CPD directly to performance management, with its emphasis on a clear focus and purpose with appropriate outcomes leading to sustained impact on classroom practice and set against the standards framework. They can also ensure that CPD remains connected to the broader concerns of continuing professional learning with its emphasis on critical, analytical development focused on teaching and learning. One way to do this is for schools/colleges to adopt revised structures for CPD that accommodate initial training and induction (Stages 1 and 2) and link them with early professional development (Stage 3) and other stages of professional career-long learning through to school leadership and beyond (Stage 6). This kind of initiative allows schools/colleges to regard professional development as an integral part of school development thereby making explicit as CPD all aspects of school developmental work such as school-based curriculum, pedagogic or pastoral initiatives, practitioner research, advisory group work and providing recognition of this. It also allows CPD to be linked directly to life-long learning and performance management focusing on the improvement of teaching and learning, and the raising of attainment.

Research findings indicate a number of considerations that schools/colleges at the cutting edge of induction practice are grappling with in order to ensure that the new teacher's induction experience and subsequent CPD activities foster professional development in relation to the inter-relationship between professional values and personal commitment, professional knowledge and understanding, and professional skills and abilities. These include:

- the balance within early professional development, given institutional needs, between the professional development of the teacher and the needs of the pupils; the balance within the learning organisation of teacher learning and pupil learning.
- the balance in early professional development between an emphasis on evidence-led development of teachers' knowledge and skills focused on teaching and learning within the standards framework and critical, analytical development focused on the clarification of what constitutes reflective practice and 'scholarship in teaching' in a variety of contexts (see Boyer 1990).
- the appropriate integration of information and communications technology into the early professional development profile of teachers.
- the best use of lesson observation and feedback to stimulate self-review and constructive criticism and to strengthen pedagogical skills.
- the most productive participation in networking – actual and virtual – with other schools and colleges to gain wider experience of the challenges of teaching and also insights into new ideas and approaches.
- the most effective way to engage with research and enquiry into the dynamics of the teaching and learning process.

- the kind of support that will facilitate high-quality coaching and mentoring for new teachers from more experienced teachers and encourage collaborative work with other teaching colleagues in which the NQTs' contribution and potential leadership is both recognised and valued.
- the selection of appropriate 'Masterclasses' for new teachers to attend in a variety of specific areas relevant to their needs – such as behaviour management, special needs, teaching EAL children, working with gifted and talented children, working with other trained adults in the classroom, developing thinking skills, accelerated learning, etc.
- the effective use of evidence of pupils' learning in assessing teachers' professional development.
- the use of more holistic quality indicators to support judgements made when reviewers are discussing progress with new teachers or completing their assessment reports, for example, the NQT:
  - having sought the respect of pupils in classes taught,
  - having a purposeful class ethos,
  - being valued by other members of staff,
  - making a contribution at the whole-school level,
  - being trusted by parents or guardians, and
  - enabling pupils to make good progress.

## What best practice looks like in this developing area

Some aspects of continuing professional development were highlighted by the research as needing further attention if educators want to encourage good practice. In terms of providing a bridge from ITE to induction, everyone agreed that the statutory induction arrangements did make a bridge into induction and the first year of teaching. But induction needs to combine both professional and managerial considerations in a balanced whole if it is to serve to reinforce new teachers' sense of being integrated in the professional culture of schools rather than just being absorbed into other people's agendas. The following are examples of best practice currently operating in schools:

- where possible, initial induction meetings are arranged before the NQTs begin work in the school,
- the school staff, as a whole, is conscious of the needs of the NQT for training and support,
- opportunities are provided for a wide range of staff to have input into NQT induction, however informal.

The induction arrangements are also designed to form a bridge from induction to the second year of teaching and beyond. Here they appear to be less successful in the view of induction tutors and NQTs themselves and probably need to be augmented by an early professional development strategy as being piloted in a number of LEAs at present. Nevertheless, the statutory induction arrangements have proved to be versatile and have slotted well into the whole teacher career structure, including performance management and CPD. Support, monitoring and assessment are all contained in induction so it brings in all three elements of performance management in an anticipatory way that facilitates smooth transition into professional frameworks and ways of working. These are some of the traits that can help to provide a sure foundation for NQTs' transition from induction into the established teaching positions of their second and subsequent years:

- schools provide a programme of induction-related activities phased throughout the induction period, including all the statutory elements and elements found most useful to NQTs,
- the programme has specific CPD content that reflects anticipated roles and responsibilities likely to be assumed by NQTs early on in their career development,
- observation of good teachers, both in the school and beyond, is routinely arranged, with opportunities for discussions afterwards, as this is the foundation upon which all future CPD depends,
- CPD and assessment are given coherence and continuity through a Professional Development Portfolio, which embodies the wider idea of the autonomous professional. Sections may include the Career Entry Profile, objectives, records of observations of a new teacher's teaching and observations by him or her of experienced teachers, records of target setting and reviewing meetings, assessment forms and the Professional Development record, which in turn can be linked to a credit-bearing scheme leading to accreditation.

In relation to the wider context of teachers' responsibility for their own learning, if professional development is regarded as a holistic process, then putting the emphasis on induction arrangements as self-directed rather than imposed helps NQTs appreciate the issues involved in taking charge of their own professional development. Some ways to facilitate this include:

- schools with large numbers of NQTs appointing a senior person to coordinate the work of other staff and providing monitoring and training specifically related to the induction process and assessment procedures, including knowledge and understanding of induction standards.
- all staff involved in induction being trained to assess NQTs against the standards. This training needs to be regularly reviewed and, where

possible, made continuous with training in assessing standards in initial training and performance management. In this way teachers become adept at making judgements about the quality of teaching and learning and the various factors involved in supporting and facilitating it professionally.

- schools/colleges setting up a training group to meet regularly to discuss issues around mentoring, assessment, support and guidance and to share good practice. The group is led by an appropriate senior teacher in the school and is seen as being part and parcel of the ethos of being a 'learning institution'. When linked to collaboration with local schools, LEA advisers, higher education institutions, governors, parents and others in the local community, the school thereby generates a 'learning community' and communicates a commitment to continuing improvement.

## Conclusion

Teaching is a complex and subtle activity, a special kind of generative and communicative art which seeks to get the experiences of learning underway and to sustain them in practice. Classrooms are places where multiple interactions, interpretations and responses occur. This is so because the experience of teaching and learning involves not merely the transfer of knowledge championed by conservatives nor the cultural interplay championed by progressives, but more crucially a courtship of sensibility inherent in and a vital feature of human understanding itself. As new teachers work towards achieving the induction standards and confirmation of QTS, they undoubtedly need guidance and support to address specific development needs and sometimes to prepare themselves to take on additional responsibilities early in their career. This can best be provided through well-structured induction programmes that build on their initial training and provide a secure basis for NQTs being regarded by their pupils and their peers as established teachers.

But new teachers also need a range of experiences which will enable them to develop further professionally in relation to the full gamut of roles and responsibilities they will be expected to assume as part of their work as a teacher. Usually the most important source of development opportunities will be the experience of doing the day-to-day job, along with support arrangements provided by colleagues in the school, especially their induction tutor. However, the value of discussing and sharing their successes and concerns about work should not be underestimated. This can sometimes be facilitated in terms of assisting both professional development and personal growth through formal CPD opportunities that could be school-based or offered through local authorities or other agencies such as university departments of education and the like. The ultimate purpose of

CPD, as we have defined it, is not confined to meeting the immediate needs of the new teacher but also instilling in them a sense that learning is an integral part of professional practice. For, as the GTC rightly admonishes, 'professional learning enables teachers to interpret and respond to the changing demands of practice and exercise their professional judgement in informed and creative ways' (GTC 2000: 1).

Teachers contribute fundamentally to the quality of society and to its future well-being. The role of the teacher will become more complex and more important still as the nature of knowledge and information changes under the influence of the growing presence of information and communications technology. Teachers will act as gatekeepers to the knowledge and to the powers of discernment and discrimination which will help those who gain it to use it wisely and for the good of others. Therefore, while new members of the profession should be able to demonstrate high standards, they must also be helped to develop versatility in their exercise of skills so as to work creatively with both the universals of learning and the individual particularities of learners. It is here that the continuity of development, so often proclaimed as a principal aim of induction, needs to be realised so as to provide the 'appropriate circumstances' (Tickle 2000b) for early professional development that will put within reach 'the world-class teacher in world-class schools' (Morris 2001: 1) to which we all aspire.

# Bibliography

Association of Teachers and Lecturers (1999) *Induction – Bridge or Barrier?* London: ATL.

Baker, K. and Earley, P. (1989) 'The Demand for Supply', *Education*, 173:18, 426–427.

Baker, L. (1992) *Preparation, Induction and Support for Newly Appointed Head-teachers and Deputy Heads*, Slough: EMIE.

Barnard, N. (1999) 'Schools Fail to Give Induction Training', *Times Educational Supplement*, 22 October.

Barrington, R. (2000) *An Investigation into the Induction Period Which Considers the Perspectives of NQTs and Their Induction Tutor*, paper presented at British Educational Research Association conference, Cardiff, September 2000.

BBC (2001) *Teacher Shortages Worst For Ages*, BBC News: 28 August. URL: http://news.bbc.co.uk/hi/english/education/newsid_1512000/1512590.stm [accessed 5/12/01].

Bennett, N. and Carr, C. (1993) *Learning to Teach*, London: Routledge.

Bines, H. and Boydell, D. (1995) 'Managing Support for Newly Qualified Teachers in Primary Schools', *Mentoring and Tutoring*, 3:1, 57–61.

Bishop, P., Sands, M. and Biddulph, M. (1992) 'A Bridge Between Training and Induction', *New Era in Education*, 73:1, 23–26.

Blake, D. and Hill, D. (1995) 'The Newly Qualified Teacher in School', *Research Papers in Education*, 10:3, 309–339.

Bleach, K. (1998) 'Off to a Flying Start? Induction Procedures for Newly Qualified Teachers in Secondary Schools in the Republic of Ireland', *Mentoring and Tutoring*, 6:1–2, 55–65.

Bleach, K. (1999) *The Induction and Mentoring of Newly Qualified Teachers*, London: David Fulton.

Bleach, K. (2000) *The Newly Qualified Secondary Teacher's Handbook*, London: David Fulton.

Bolam, R. (1995) 'The Induction of Newly Qualified Teachers in Schools: Where Next?', *British Journal of In-Service Education*, 21:3, 247–272.

Bolam, R., Taylor, J. and British Association for the Advancement of Science (1972) *The Induction and Guidance of Beginning Teachers*, Leicester: BAAS.

Bolton, E. (1993) 'Education and Culture'. Presidential Address to the North of England Education Conference, Blackpool (6–8 January).

Boyer, E. (1990) *Scholarship Reconsidered*. Princeton, NJ: Carnegie Foundation for the Advancement of Teaching.

Brading, M. (1999) *Induction of Newly Qualified Teachers: Perception of the Professional Development of NQTS as Described by New Teachers, Their Mentors and Headteachers*, BERA Conference, Brighton, 1999.

Bridges, D. and Kerry, T. (1993*) Developing Teachers Professionally: Reflections for Initial and In-Service Trainers*, London: Routledge.

Brock, B. and Grady, M. (1997) *From First Year to First Rate: Principles Guiding Beginning Teachers*, London: Sage.

Brown, K. (2001) 'Mentoring and the Retention of Newly Qualified Language Teachers', *Cambridge Journal of Education*, 31:1, 69–77.

Bubb, S. (2000a) 'Caution: Danger Ahead – the Induction Standards', *Times Educational Supplement*, Friday, 14 January, 3–4.

Bubb, S. (2000b) *Statutory Induction – a Fair Deal for All?* (Viewpoint series No. 12), London: Institute of Education.

Bubb, S. (2000c) *The Effective Induction of Newly Qualified Primary Teachers: An Induction Tutor's Handbook*, London: David Fulton.

Bubb, S. (2001a) *A Newly Qualified Teacher's Manual: How to Meet the Induction Standards*, London: David Fulton.

Bubb, S. (2001b) 'QTS Confusion Needs Qualification', *Times Educational Supplement*, 23 February, 31.

Bubb, S. and Hoare, P. (2001) *Performance Management: Monitoring Teaching in the Primary School*, London: David Fulton.

Bullough, R. (1989) *First-Year Teacher: A Case Study*, New York: Teachers College Press.

Bullough, R., Knowles, J. and Crow, N. (1991) *Emerging as a Teacher*, London: Routledge.

Cains, R. and Brown, C. (1998) 'Newly Qualified Teachers: A Comparative Analysis of the Perceptions held by B Ed and PGCE-trained Primary Teachers of the Level and Frequency of Stress Experienced During the First Year of Teaching', *Educational Psychology*, 18:1, 97–110.

Calderhead, J. and Lambert, J. (1992) *The Induction of Newly-Appointed Teachers*, London: GTC.

Calderhead, J. and Shorrock, S. (1997) *Understanding Teacher Education: Case Studies in the Professional Development of Beginning Teachers*, London: Falmer.

Capel, S. (1998) 'The Transition From Student Teacher to Newly Qualified Teacher: Some Findings', *Journal of In-Service Education*, 24:3, 393–409.

Capel, S., Leask, M. and Turner, T. (1997) *Starting to Teach in the Secondary School: A Companion for the Newly Qualified Teacher*, London: Routledge.

Carre, C. (1993) 'The First Year of Teaching', in Bennett, N. and Carre, C. (eds) *Learning to Teach*, London, Routledge.

Codell, E. (1999) *Education Esme: Diary of a Teacher's First Year*, Chapel Hill, NC: Algonquin Books.

Cowley, S. (1999) *Starting Teaching. How to Succeed and Survive*, London: Cassell Education.

Cross, R. (1995) 'The Role of the Mentor in Utilising the Support System for the Newly Qualified Teacher', *School Organisation*, 15:1, 35–42.

Dallat, J., Moran, A. and Abbott, L. (1999) 'External Support for Newly Qualified

Teachers: Induction Officers' Views Explored', *Research in Education*, 62, 41–54.

D'Arcy, J. (1988) *The First Years of Teaching*, Belfast: [S.I]: Northern Ireland Council for Educational Research.

Department for Education (1992) *Circular 9/92: Initial Teacher Training (Secondary Phase)*, London: DfE.

Department for Education (1992) *Induction for Newly Qualified Teachers*, London: HMSO.

Department for Education and Employment (1997) *Excellence in Schools*, London: DfEE.

Department for Education and Employment (1998a) *Induction for New Teachers – A Consultation Document*, London: DfEE.

Department for Education and Employment (1998b) *Reducing the Bureaucratic Burden*, London: DfEE.

Department for Education and Employment (1998c) *Teaching: High Status High Standards. Circular 4/98*, London: DfEE.

Department for Education and Employment (1999) *Circular 5/99: The Induction Period for Newly Qualified Teachers*, London: DfEE.

Department for Education and Employment (2000a) *Circular 90/2000: The Induction Period for Newly Qualified Teachers*, London: DfEE.

Department for Education and Employment (2000b) *Performance Management Model Policy*, London: DfEE.

Department for Education and Employment (2000c) *School Teachers' Pay and Conditions*, London: DfEE.

Department for Education and Employment (2001) *The Standards Fund 2001–2002*, London: DfEE.

Department of Education for Northern Ireland (1991) *Teachers for the Twenty First Century: A Review of Initial Teacher Training*, Bangor, County Down: Deni.

Department for Education and Skills (2001a) 'Induction Funding for NQTs – Numeracy Tests'. Letter to LEAs, 7 August. Darlington, DfES

Department for Education and Skills (2001b) *Guidance 0649/2001: Helping You Develop: Guidance on Producing a Professional Development Record*, London: DfES.

Department for Education and Skills (2001c) *Continuing Professional Development Strategy*, London: DfES.

Department for Education and Skills (2001d) *Learning and Teaching*, London: DfES.

Department for Education and Skills (2001e) *The Standards' Framework*, London: DfES.

Department for Education and Skills (2001f) *Circular 582/2001: The Induction Period for Newly Qualified Teachers*, London: DfEE.

Department of Education and Science Inspectorate of Schools (1982) *The New Teacher in School*, London: HMSO.

Department of Education and Science Inspectorate of Schools (1992) *The Induction and Probation of New Teachers, 1988–1991: A Report by HMI*, London: DES.

Dollas, R. (1992) *Voices of Beginning Teachers: Visions and Realities*, New York: Teachers College Press.

Draper, J. *et al.* (1997) *Probationers on Supply: A GTC Report on the Needs of Probationer Teachers on Supply*, Edinburgh: GTC.

Draper, J., Fraser, H. and Taylor, W. (1991) *A Study of Probationers*, Edinburgh [S.I]: Moray House, Institute of Education and Heriot-Watt University.

Draper, J., Fraser, H. and Taylor, W. (1992) *A Study of Probationer Teachers*, Edinburgh: Scottish Office Education Department, Research and Intelligence Unit.

Earley, P. (1993) 'Initiation Rights? Beginning Teachers' Professional Development and the Objectives of Induction Training', *British Journal of In-Service Education*, 19:1, 5–11.

Earley, P. (1996) 'Competence Frameworks and Profiles for Newly Qualified Teachers', in Hustler, D. and McIntyre, D. (eds), *Developing Competent Teachers*, London: David Fulton.

Earley, P. and Kinder, K. (1994) *Initiation Rights: Effective Induction Practices for New Teachers*, Slough: NFER.

Emmerson, I. (2000) 'One Mistake and You're Out', *Times Educational Supplement*, Friday, 17 November, 30–31.

European Network on Teacher Education Policies (2001) *Coordination Note*, paper presented at Teacher Education and the role of Post-graduate studies and research in teacher reform policies, June 2001.

Furlong, J. and Maynard, T. (1995a) *Mentoring Student Teachers: A Practical Guide*, London: Falmer Press.

Furlong, J. and Maynard, T. (1995b) *Mentoring Student Teachers: the Growth of Professional Knowledge*, London: Routledge.

Furlong, J. *et al.* (2000) *Teacher Education in Transition: Re-forming Professionalism*, Buckingham: Oxford University Press.

Further Education Funding Council (2001) *The Induction of Newly Qualified Teachers in Sixth Form Colleges*, Darlington: DfEE.

General Teaching Council (1990) *The Management of Probation*, London: GTC.

General Teaching Council (2000) *Draft Professional Learning Framework: The General Teaching Council's Professional Learning Framework – a Draft for Discussion and Development*, London: GTC.

Geva-May, I. and Dori, Y. (1996) 'Analysis of an Induction Model', *British Journal of In-Service Education*, 22:3, 235–356.

Gloucestershire Education Department (1999) *The Induction Period for Newly Qualified Teachers: A Handbook for Induction Tutors*, Gloucestershire: ED.

Goddard, B. (1993) 'The Role of the LEA in Induction', *British Journal of In-Service Education,* 19:1, 46–54.

Greiner-Makin, S. (1996) 'Why is the Duckling Preferable to the Parrot as a Teacher? Four Beginning Teacher Types', *European Journal of Teacher Education*, 19:1, 13–18.

Hagger, H. and White, A. (1995) *Profile for Professional Development: Induction of Newly Qualified Teachers*, Oxford: Oxfordshire Education Department.

Hammersley, M. (1997) 'Educational Research and Teaching: a Response to David Hargreaves – Teacher Training Agency Lecture', *British Educational Research Journal*, 23:2, 141–161.

Hargreaves, D. (1998) *Creative Professionalism: The Role of Teachers in the Knowledge Society*, London: Demos.

Hayes, D. (2000) *The Handbook for Newly Qualified Teachers: Meeting the Standards in Primary and Middle Schools*, London: David Fulton.

Heilbronn, R. and Jones, C. (1997) *New Teachers in an Urban Comprehensive*, Stoke on Trent: Trentham Books.

Hextall, I. and Mahony, P. (1999) *'Modernising' the Teacher*, paper presented at the European Conference on Educational Research, Lahti, Finland.

Hill, B., Dobson, K. and Riches, C. (1977) *The Professional Tutor: A Bibliography on Inservice Training, Probation and School Practice, Supervision, and Staff Development*, Hatfield: Hatfield Polytechnic.

Hillage, J. (1998) *Excellence in Research on Schools*, London: Institute for Employment Studies.

HMI (1993) *The New Teacher in School: a Survey by HM Inspectors in England and Wales 1992*, Great Britain: Department for Education Inspectorate of Schools.

Holmes, E. (1999) *Handbook for Newly Qualified Teachers: The Definitive Guide to Your First Year of Teaching*, London: The Stationery Office.

Horne, M. (2001a) 'Shortage could last forever,' *Times Educational Supplement: News and Opinion*, 31 August.

Horne, M. (2001b) *Classroom Assistance: Why Teachers Must Transform Teaching*, London: DEMOS.

Howson, J. (2001) 'Young Guns Are Going For It', *Times Educational Supplement*, 2 March, 24.

Irish National Teachers' Organisation (1992) *Information Booklet for Teachers in Non-Permanent Teaching Posts*, Dublin: The Organisation.

James, E. (1972) *The James Report*, London: DFE.

Jones, L., Reid, D. and Bevins, S. (1997) 'Teachers' Perceptions of Mentoring in a Collaborative Model of Initial Teacher Training', *Journal of Education for Teaching*, 23: 253–261,

Jones, M. (2001) 'Mentors' Perceptions of their Roles in School-based Teacher in England and Germany', *Journal of Education for Teaching*, 27:1, 75–94.

King, S. (2000) *Theory into Practice: Into the Black Box – Observing Classes*, Sheffield: Geographical Association.

Koetsier, C. and Wubbels, T. (1995) 'Bridging the Gap Between Initial Teacher Training and Teacher Induction', *Journal of Education for Teaching*, 21:3, 333–345.

Kyriacou, C. (1993) 'Research in the Development of Expertise in Classroom Teaching during Initial Teacher Training and the First Year of Teaching', *Education Review*, 45, 79–87.

Lee, B. (2000) *Continuing Professional Development: Teachers' Perspectives. A Summary*, Slough: NFER.

Lewis, P. and Varley, S. (2000) 'Monitoring the Induction Experience of Newly Qualified Teachers', paper presented at British Educational Research Association conference, Cardiff, September 2000.

McCabe, C. (1978) *Evaluation Report No.18: The Extension Year 1977–8*, University of Newcastle upon Tyne – School of Education Northumberland Induction Pilot Project.

McIntyre, J. and Byrd, D. (1996) *Preparing Tomorrow's Teachers: The Field Experience*, Thousand Oaks, CA: Corwin.

McLeod, C. (2000) 'The Career Entry Profile as an Induction Tool', *Professional Development Today*, Summer, 39–48.

McNair, A. (1944) *The McNair Report: Teachers and Youth Leaders*, London: HMSO.

Mahoney, P. (1996) 'Competence and the First Year of Teaching', in Hustler, D. and McIntyre, D. (eds) *Developing Competent Teachers*, London: David Fulton.

Marshall, C. (2000) 'Policy Discourse Analysis: Negotiating Gender Equity', *Journal of Education Policy*, 15:2, 125–156.

Mason, M. (2000) 'Teachers as Critical Mediators of Knowledge', *Journal of Philosophy of Education*, 34:2, 343–352.

Maynard, T. (2000) 'Learning to Teach or Learning to Manage Mentors? Experiences of School-based Teacher Training', *Mentoring and Tutoring*, 8:1, 17–30.

Menter, I. (1995) 'What Newly Qualified Teachers Really Need: Evidence from a Support Group', *Journal of Teacher Development*, 4:3, 14–21.

Merry, R., Moyles, J., Chapman, L., Hislam, J., Kitson, N., Hunter-Carsch, M. and Suschitzky, W. (2000) 'Entering the Lion's Den! Experiences of Entrants in the First Year of Primary Teaching', paper presented at British Educational Research Association conference, Cardiff, September.

Morant, R. (1974) *The Objectives of Teacher Induction: An Occasional Paper*, Crewe: The author.

Morris, E. (2001) *Professionalism and Trust – the Future of Teachers and Teaching*, London: DfES/Social Market Foundation.

Moyles, J., Suschitsky, W. and Chapman, L. (1999) 'Mentoring in Primary Schools: Ethos, Sturcture and Workload', *Journal of In-Service Education*, 25:1, 161–171.

Mulholland, J. and Wallace, J. (2001) 'Teacher Induction and Elementary Science Teaching: Enhancing Self-Efficiency', *Teaching and Teacher Education*, 17:2, 243–261.

National Foundation for Educational Research (2000) *The LEA Contribution to School Improvement – a Role Worth Fighting For*, London: Local Government Association. URL: www.lga.gov.uk/lga/education/ [accessed 20/8/01].

National Primary Centre (1994) *The Open Door: What Makes Mentoring Work, Exploring the Roles and Relationships of Mentors and Newly-Qualified Teachers in Primary Schools*, Oxford: NPC.

National Primary Centre (1998) *Brace Yourself!: Information to Help Newly Qualified Teachers Prepare for their First Appointment*, Oxford: National Primary Centre.

National Union of Teachers (2000a) *Short-changing the Teaching Profession? The Report of a Survey of Central Government and LEA Funding of Induction for Newly Qualified Teachers in England During 1999–2000*, London: NUT.

National Union of Teachers (2000b) *A Helping Hand – the Role of the Induction Tutors*, London: NUT.

National Union of Teachers (2001a) *Crossing the Winning Line or Falling at the First Hurdle?* London: NUT.

National Union of Teachers (2001b) *A Guide to Induction for Newly Qualified Teachers*, NUT.

Newman, C. (2000) 'Seeds of Professional Development in Pre-service Teachers: A Study of their Dreams and Goals', *International Journal of Educational Research*, 33:2, 125–217.

Newton, L. (1991) 'What Comes Next? The In-service Needs of Newly Qualified Primary Teachers', *British Journal of In-Service Education*, 17:1, 75–80.

Oberski, I. (1999) 'The Importance of Relationships in Teacher Education', *Journal of Education for Teaching*, 25:2, 135–150.

OFSTED (1999) *Handbook for Inspecting Primary and Nursery Schools*, London, The Stationery Office.

OFSTED (2001a) *The Annual Report of Her Majesty's Chief Inspector of Schools*, London: The Stationery Office.

OFSTED (2001b) *Inspection of LEAs: Grade Criteria for Inspection Judgements*, London: OFSTED.

OFSTED (2001c) *The Induction of Newly Qualified Teachers*, London: OFSTED.

O'Hara, M. (2000) *Teaching 3–8: Meeting the Standards for Initial Teacher Training and Induction*, London: Continuum.

Pennington, M. (1996) *Learning to Teach in Hong Kong: The First Year in the Classroom*, Hong Kong: City University of Hong Kong, Department of English.

Powney, J. (1997) 'Career Entry Profiles: Lessons from the Pilot', *Professional Development Today*, 1:1, 9–13.

Pring, R. (2000a) *Philosophy of Educational Research*, London and New York: Continuum.

Pring, R. (2000b) 'The "False Dualism" of Educational Research', *Journal of the Philosophy of Education*, 34:2, 247–260.

Reynolds, A., Tannenbaum, R. and Rosenfeld, M. (1992) *Beginning Teacher Knowledge of General Principles of Teaching and Learning: A National Survey*, Princeton, NJ: Educational Testing Service.

Richards, C. (2000) 'You Don't Have to be a Genius, But …', *Times Educational Supplement – Letters*, 7 January.

Rosenfeld, M., Freeberg, N. and Bukatko, P. (1992) *The Professional Functions of Secondary Schools*, Princeton, N.J.

Russell, M. (2001) 'QTS Confusion Needs Qualification', *Times Educational Supplement*, 23 February, p.31.

Schilling, C. (1991) 'Supply Teachers: Working on the Margins', *Educational Research*, 33, 3–11.

Self-Help Action Plan for Education Project (1992) *Colleges and Schools' INSET Policy on Induction of New Lecturers and Teachers and their Professional Development*, Unpublished.

Sidgwick, S. (1996) 'Government Policy and the Induction of New Teachers', in McBride, R. (ed.) *Teacher Education Policy: Some Issues Arising from Research and Practice*, London: Falmer Press, 97–112.

Simco, N. (1995) 'Professional Profiling and Development in the Induction Year', *British Journal of In-Service Education*, 19:1, 3–4.

Simco, N. (2000) *Succeeding in the Induction Year*, Exeter: Learning Matters.

Simco, N. and Sixsmith, S. (1999) *The TTA's Career Entry Profile: is ITT and Induction Now Seamless?* Paper presented at BERA, Sussex, 2001.

Sinclair, A. (1999) *How to Succeed in an Inner-City Classroom: A Guide for New Teachers*, London: Bell Publications.

Smith, P. and West-Burnham, J. (1993) *Mentoring in the Effective School*, Harlow: Longman.

Spear, M. and Lee, B. (2000) *Who Would Be a Teacher? A Review of Factors Motivating and Demotivating Prospective and Practising Teachers*, Slough: NFER.

Spindler, J. and Biott, C. (2000) 'Target Setting in the Induction of Newly Qualified Teachers: Emerging Colleagueship in a Context of Performance Management', *Educational Research*, 42:3, 275–285.

Stammers, P. (1993) 'Maintaining the First Year Dream', *British Journal of In-Service Education*, 19:1, 29–35.

Swan, B. (1997) 'An Evaluation of Induction Procedures for Newly Appointed Teachers: A Study of One School', *Irish Educational Studies*, 16, 55–68.

Tabberer, R. (2000) *Supporting Induction to the Teaching Profession*, paper presented at the TTA / LGA Conference 2000, 23 March.

Teacher Training Agency (1998) *Interim Findings on the Monitoring and Support Activities for Newly Qualified Teachers in the Induction Credit Feasibility Study*, London: TTA.

Teacher Training Agency (1999a) *Supporting Induction for Newly Qualified Teachers. Part 1: Overview*, London: TTA.

Teacher Training Agency (1999b) *Supporting Induction for Newly Qualified Teachers. Part 2: Support and Monitoring*, London: TTA.

Teacher Training Agency (1999c) *Supporting Induction for Newly Qualified Teachers. Part 2: Assessment*, London: TTA.

Teacher Training Agency (1999d) *Supporting Induction for Newly Qualified Teachers. Part 4: Quality Assurance*, London: TTA.

Teacher Training Agency (2000) *Career Entry Profile,* London: TTA.

Teacher Training Agency (2001a) LEA Induction Coordinators Closed Website: www.canteach.gov.uk/leainduct.

Teacher Training Agency (2001b) *The Role of Induction Tutor: Principals and Guidance*, London: TTA.

Teacher Training Agency (2001c) *Guidance on Career Entry Profile.* London: TTA.

Thompson, M. (1991) 'Induction: A View from the Teachers' Organisation', *British Journal of In-Service Education*, 17, 229–235.

Tickett, A. (2001) 'How Was It For You?' *Professional Development Today*, 2001, 13–17.

Tickle, L. (1994) *The Induction of New Teachers: Reflective Professional Practice*, London: Cassell.

Tickle, L. (2000a) *Teacher Induction: The Way Ahead*, Buckingham: Oxford University Press.

Tickle, L. (2000b) 'Teacher Probation Resurrected: England 1999–2000', *Journal of Education Policy*, 15:6, 701–713.

Times Educational Supplement Staffroom (2001) URL: www.tes.co.uk/staffroom/ [Accessed 20/8/01].

Tooley, J. and Darby, D. (1998) *Educational Research: An OFSTED Critique*, London: OFSTED.

Totterdell, M.S. (2001) 'Educational Leadership and Teachers' Emotional Welfare: Reflections on the Contemporary School as a 'Managed' Workplace', in Wen, S. (ed.) *Aspects of School Leadership and Management in Two Island Cultures*, Taipei: Taiwan College Press.

Traquair, N. (1994) *The Open Door. What Makes Mentoring Work: Exploring the*

*Roles and Relationships of Mentors and Newly Qualified Teachers in Primary Schools*, Oxford: National Primary Centre.

Trethowan, D. and Smith, D. (1989) *Induction*, London: Industrial Society.

Turner, M. (1993) 'The Complementary Roles of the Head Teacher, the Mentor and the Advisory Teacher in Induction and School-based Teacher Training', *Mentoring*, 1:2, 30–36.

Turner, M. (1994) 'The Management of the Induction of Newly Qualified Teachers in Primary Schools', *Journal of Education for Teaching*, 20:3, 229–236.

Turner, M. and Bash, L. (1999) *Sharing Expertise in Teacher Education*, London: Cassell.

Whiting, C., Whitty, G., Furlong, J., Miles, S. and Barton, L. (1996) *Modes of Teacher Education Project: Partnership in Initial Teacher Education: a Topography*, London: Institute of Education.

Wideen, M., Mayer-Smith, J. and Moon, B. (1998) 'A Critical Analysis of the Research on Learning to Teach: Making the Case for an Ecological Perspective on Inquiry', *Review of Educational Research*, 68: 2, 130–178.

Williams, A. and Prestage, S. (2000) *Still in at the Deep End? Developing Strategies for the Induction of New Teachers*, London: Association of Teachers and Lecturers.

Wootton, M. (1992) *Assessing a New Teacher's Performance: A Checklist*, Upminster: Nightingale Teaching Consultancy.

Wright, N. (1997) 'Perceptions of Professionalism by the Mentors of Student Teachers', *Journal of Education for Teaching*, 23:3, 235–251.

# Index